Table of Contents

Free Gift

Up to 1000 delicious and healthy recipes from cooking traditions all around the world.

Please follow this link to get instant access to your Free Cookbook:
http://bookretailseller.pro/

Introduction

Why is a Paleo diet one of the healthiest ones in the world? Why should you opt for such an amazing diet? Well, we are here to tell you all that!

A Paleo diet is a healthy way of living that doesn't allow you to consume any legumes, beans, alcohol, starches, dairy products and artificial ingredients.
On the other hand, a Paleo diet allows you to consume a lot of fruits, veggies, meat, poultry, fish, seafood, nuts, seeds and healthy oils.
As you can see for yourself, a Paleo diet is a very easy one! It doesn't deprive you of your favorite foods! It just helps you consume healthier ones!
All in all, a Paleo diet helps you become a happy and healthy person that enjoys living and the world around him!

Today, we thought you could enjoy even more your Paleo diet! How?
It's so easy! You just have to combine your Paleo diet with one of the best cooking methods ever: slow cooking!
Yes, you've heard it right! Slow cooking is one of the healthiest cooking methods these days that allows you to make special dishes in no time!
So, what better idea than combining Paleo meals with slow cooking?
Trust us! It will be the best culinary experience you'll ever enjoy!

So, don't wait too long! Start a new Paleo life today and start cooking the best Paleo meals in your slow cooker from now on!
Have a lot of fun and enjoy your new and improved life!

Paleo Slow Cooker Breakfast Recipes

Apple Butter

Preparation time: 10 minutes
Cooking time: 8 hours
Servings: 10

Ingredients:
- Juice of 1 lemon
- 1 teaspoon allspice
- 1 teaspoon clove, ground
- 1 teaspoon ginger powder
- 3 pounds apples, peeled, cored and chopped
- 1 tablespoon cinnamon, ground
- 1 and ½ cups water
- ¼ teaspoon nutmeg, ground
- 1 cup maple syrup

Directions:
1. In your slow cooker, mix apples with water, lemon juice, allspice, clove, ginger powder, cinnamon, maple syrup and nutmeg.
2. Stir, cover and cook on Low for 8 hours.
3. Leave your mix to cool down for 10 minutes, blend using an immersion blender and pour into small jars.
4. Serve for breakfast!

Enjoy!

Nutrition: calories 150, fat 3, fiber 1, carbs 4, protein 3

Delicious Breakfast Bowls

Preparation time: 10 minutes
Cooking time: 8 hours
Servings: 4

Ingredients:
- ½ cup almonds, soaked for 12 hours and drained
- ½ cup walnuts, soaked for 12 hours and drained
- 2 apples, peeled, cored and cubed
- 1 butternut squash, peeled and cubed
- 1 teaspoon cinnamon powder
- 1 tablespoon coconut sugar
- ½ teaspoon nutmeg, ground
- 1 cup coconut milk
- Maple syrup for serving

Directions:
1. Put almonds and walnuts in your blender, add some of the soaking water, blend really well and transfer to your slow cooker.
2. Add apples, squash, cinnamon, coconut sugar, nutmeg and coconut milk, stir, cover and cook on Low for 8 hours.
3. Use a potato masher to mash the whole mix, divide into bowls and serve.

Enjoy!

Nutrition: calories 140, fat 1, fiber 2, carbs 2, protein 5

Tasty Veggie Frittata

Preparation time: 10 minutes
Cooking time: 2 hours
Servings: 4

Ingredients:

- Cooking spray
- 6 eggs
- 4 ounces mushrooms, chopped
- 1 teaspoon garlic powder
- A pinch of black pepper
- ¼ cup spinach, chopped
- 2 green onions, chopped
- ¼ cup cherry tomatoes, chopped
- 1 teaspoon olive oil

Directions:

1. Spray your slow cooker with cooking spray and leave aside for now.
2. Heat up a pan with the oil over medium heat; add onions, spinach, mushrooms and tomatoes, stir and sauté for a couple of minutes.
3. Transfer this to your slow cooker, add eggs, a pinch of pepper and garlic powder, stir gently, cover and cook on High for 2 hours.
4. Divide between plates and serve hot.

Enjoy!

Nutrition: calories 140, fat 2, fiber 2, carbs 4, protein 4

Hearty Breakfast Pork Mix

Preparation time: 10 minutes
Cooking time: 8 hours
Servings: 4

Ingredients:

- 1 medium pork butt
- 1 teaspoon coriander, ground
- 1 tablespoon oregano, dried
- 1 tablespoon cumin powder
- 2 tablespoons chili powder
- 2 onions, chopped
- A pinch of black pepper
- 1 teaspoon lime juice
- 4 eggs, already fried
- 2 avocados, peeled, pitted and sliced

Directions:

1. In a bowl, mix pork butt with coriander, oregano, cumin, chili powder, onions and a pinch of black pepper, rub well, transfer to your slow cooker and cook on Low for 8 hours.
2. Shred meat, divide between plates and serve with fried eggs and avocado slices on top and with lime juice all over.

Enjoy!

Nutrition: calories 220, fat 2, fiber 2, carbs 6, protein 2

Delicious Sausage and Eggs Casserole

Preparation time: 10 minutes
Cooking time: 5 hours
Servings: 6

Ingredients:
- 1 broccoli head, florets separated
- 10 eggs, whisked
- 12 ounces sausages, cooked and sliced
- 2 garlic cloves, minced
- A pinch of sea salt
- Cooking spray
- Black pepper to the taste

Directions:
1. Spray your slow cooker with the cooking spray and layer half of the broccoli florets.
2. Add a layer of sausages, and then add half of the whisked eggs, a pinch of salt and some black pepper.
3. Add garlic, the rest of the broccoli, sausages and the rest of the eggs.
4. Cover and cook on Low for 5 hours.
5. Leave casserole to cool down, slice, divide between plates and serve.

Enjoy!

Nutrition: calories 200, fat 3, fiber 3, carbs 6, protein 2

Special Breakfast Delight

Preparation time: 10 minutes
Cooking time: 6 hours and 10 minutes
Servings: 4

Ingredients:
- 1 and 1/3 cups leek, chopped
- 2 tablespoons coconut oil
- 1 cup kale, chopped
- 2 teaspoons garlic, minced
- 8 eggs
- 2/3 cup sweet potato, grated
- 1 and ½ cups beef sausage, casings removed and chopped

Directions:
1. Heat up a pan with the oil over medium high heat, add leek, stir and cook for 1 minute.
2. Add garlic, sweet potatoes and kale, stir, cook for 2 minutes more and transfer to your slow cooker.
3. Add eggs and sausage meat, stir everything, cover and cook on Low for 6 hours.
4. Leave this tasty mix to cool down before slicing and serving it for breakfast.

Enjoy!

Nutrition: calories 190, fat 2, fiber 2, carbs 6, protein 10

Delicious Mexican Breakfast

Preparation time: 10 minutes
Cooking time: 8 hours and 5 minutes
Servings: 4

Ingredients:
- 1 sweet potato, grated
- ½ cup bacon, chopped
- 8 eggs, whisked
- 1 red bell pepper, chopped
- 1 yellow onion, chopped
- 8 ounces mushrooms, chopped
- A pinch of cumin, ground
- A pinch of black pepper

Directions:
1. Heat up a pan over medium high heat, add bacon, fry until it's crispy, transfer to paper towels, drain and leave aside for now.
2. Heat up the same pan over medium high heat, add onion, stir and cook for 3 minutes.
3. Transfer this to your slow cooker; also add fried bacon, sweet potato, mushrooms, bell pepper and eggs.
4. Whisk gently, season with black pepper and cumin, cover and cook on Low for 8 hours.
5. Leave this Mexican casserole to cool down, slice and serve it.

Enjoy!

Nutrition: calories 200, fat 4, fiber 2, carbs 7, protein 5

Special Egg Casserole

Preparation time: 10 minutes
Cooking time: 8 hours and 10 minutes
Servings: 4

Ingredients:
- 1 red onion, chopped
- 1 pound bacon, cooked and chopped
- 1 red bell pepper, chopped
- 2 medium sweet potatoes, grated
- 12 eggs
- 2 garlic cloves, minced
- 1 tablespoon coconut oil
- 1 teaspoon dill, chopped
- 1 cup coconut milk
- A pinch of red pepper, crushed
- Black pepper to the taste
- A pinch of sea salt

Directions:
1. Heat up a pan with the coconut oil over medium high heat, add garlic, bell pepper and onion, stir and cook for 5 minutes.
2. Add grated sweet potato, red pepper, black pepper and a pinch of salt, stir and cook for 2 minutes more.
3. Transfer half of this to your slow cooker and spread on the bottom.
4. In a bowl, mix eggs with coconut milk and whisk well.
5. Pour half of the eggs over the veggies, add bacon, then add another veggie layer and top with the rest of the eggs.
6. Sprinkle dill all over, cover and cook on Low for 8 hours.
7. Leave this tasty casserole to cool down before serving for breakfast.

Enjoy!

Nutrition: calories 240, fat 2, fiber 3, carbs 6, protein 8

Simple Breakfast Meatloaf

Preparation time: 10 minutes
Cooking time: 3 hours and 10 minutes
Servings: 4

Ingredients:

- 1 onion, chopped
- 2 pounds pork, minced
- 1 teaspoon red pepper flakes
- 1 teaspoon coconut oil
- 3 garlic cloves, minced
- ¼ cup almond flour
- 1 teaspoon oregano, chopped
- 1 tablespoon sage, minced
- A pinch of sea salt
- 1 tablespoon paprika
- 1 teaspoon marjoram, dried
- 2 eggs

Directions:

1. Heat up a pan with the oil over medium high heat, add onion, stir and cook for 2 minutes.
2. Add garlic, stir, cook for 2 minutes more, take off heat and leave aside to cool down.
3. In a bowl, mix pork with a pinch of salt, pepper flakes, flour, oregano, sage, paprika, marjoram and eggs and whisk everything.
4. Add garlic and onion and stir again.
5. Shape your meatloaf, transfer to your slow cooker, cover and cook on Low for 3 hours.
6. Leave aside to cool down, slice and serve.

Enjoy!

Nutrition: calories 200, fat 3, fiber 2, carbs 7, protein 10

Easy Eggs and Chorizo Breakfast

Preparation time: 10 minutes
Cooking time: 6 hours and 10 minutes
Servings: 4

Ingredients:

- 4 garlic cloves, minced
- 1 yellow onion, chopped
- 1 pound chorizo, casings removed and chopped
- 12 eggs
- 1 cup coconut milk
- 1 butternut squash, peeled and cubed
- 2 tablespoons coconut oil

Directions:

1. Heat up a pan with half of the oil over medium high heat; add onion and garlic, stir and sauté for 5 minutes.
2. Add chorizo, stir, cook for 3 minutes more and take off heat.
3. In a bowl, mix eggs with coconut milk and stir well.
4. Grease your slow cooker with the rest of the oil and add butternut squash on the bottom.
5. Add onions mix and spread as well.
6. Add eggs at the end cover and cook on Low for 6 hours.
7. Leave aside to cool down, slice and serve for breakfast.

Enjoy!

Nutrition: calories 189, fat 5, fiber 3, carbs 6, protein 7

Breakfast Apple Butter

Preparation time: 10 minutes
Cooking time: 8 hours
Servings: 8

Ingredients:
- 8 cups apples, peeled, cored and chopped
- 1 teaspoon allspice, ground
- 1 teaspoon clove, ground
- 1 teaspoon ginger powder
- Juice from 1 lemon
- 1 tablespoon cinnamon powder
- ¼ teaspoon nutmeg, ground
- 1 and ½ cups water
- 1 cup maple syrup

Directions:
1. In your slow cooker, mix apples with allspice, clove, ginger, cinnamon, nutmeg, maple syrup, water and lemon juice, stir, cover and cook on Low for 8 hours.
2. Leave your apple butter mix to cool down, blend using an immersion blender, divide into jars and serve for breakfast.

Enjoy!

Nutrition: calories 212, fat 4, fiber 6, carbs 12, protein 3

Great Veggie Breakfast Frittata

Preparation time: 10 minutes
Cooking time: 2 hours
Servings: 4

Ingredients:
- 6 eggs, whisked
- 4 ounces mushrooms, sliced
- ¼ cup spinach, chopped
- 2 green onions, chopped
- 1 teaspoon ghee
- ¼ cup cherry tomatoes, sliced
- 2 teaspoons Italian seasoning

Directions:
1. Heat up a pan with the ghee over medium high heat, add mushrooms, onions, spinach, green onions and tomatoes, stir and cook for 2-3 minutes.
2. Transfer this mix to your slow cooker, add whisked eggs, season with Italian seasoning, stir a bit, cover and cook on High for 2 hours.
3. Leave your frittata to cool down a bit, slice and serve.

Enjoy!

Nutrition: calories 200, fat 4, fiber 6, carbs 12, protein 3

Butternut Squash Breakfast Mix

Preparation time: 10 minutes
Cooking time: 8 hours
Servings: 4

Ingredients:
- 2 apples, peeled, cored and cubed
- ½ cup walnuts, soaked for 12 hours and drained
- ½ cup almonds
- 1 butternut squash, peeled and cubed
- 1 teaspoon cinnamon powder
- ½ teaspoon nutmeg, ground
- 1 tablespoon coconut sugar
- 1 cup coconut milk

Directions:
1. In your slow cooker, mix walnuts with almonds, squash cubes, apples, cinnamon, nutmeg, coconut sugar and milk, stir a bit, cover and cook on Low for 8 hours.
2. Mash using a potato masher, divide into bowls and serve for breakfast.

Enjoy!

Nutrition: calories 182, fat 3, fiber 7, carbs 14, protein 2

Breakfast Stuffed Apples

Preparation time: 10 minutes
Cooking time: 1 hour and 30 minutes
Servings: 4

Ingredients:
- ½ cup maple syrup
- ¼ cup figs, dried
- 1 teaspoon coconut sugar
- ¼ cup pecans, chopped
- 1 teaspoon lemon zest, grated
- ½ teaspoon orange zest, grated
- 1 teaspoon cinnamon powder
- ¼ teaspoon nutmeg, ground
- 1 tablespoon lemon juice
- 1 tablespoon coconut oil
- ½ cup water
- 4 apples, cored and tops cut off

Directions:
1. In a bowl, mix maple syrup with figs, coconut sugar, pecans, lemon zest, orange zest, ½ teaspoon cinnamon, nutmeg, lemon juice and coconut oil, whisk really well and stuff apples with this mix.
2. Add the water to your slow cooker, add ½ teaspoon cinnamon as well, stir, add apples inside, cover and cook on High for 1 hour and 30 minutes.
3. Divide apples between plates and serve them for breakfast.

Enjoy!

Nutrition: calories 189, fat 4, fiber 7, carbs 19, protein 2

Breakfast Apples and Sauce

Preparation time: 10 minutes
Cooking time: 4 hours
Servings: 4

Ingredients:
- 1/3 cup coconut oil, melted
- 1 tablespoon lemon juice
- ¼ cup cane juice, evaporated
- ½ teaspoon cinnamon powder
- 1 teaspoon vanilla extract
- 5 apples, cored, peeled and cubed

Directions:
1. In your instant pot mix, coconut oil with cane juice, lemon juice, cinnamon and vanilla and whisk well.
2. Add apple cubes, toss well, cover and cook on High for 4 hours.
3. Divide into bowls and serve for breakfast.

Enjoy!

Nutrition: calories 200, fat 4, fiber 6, carbs 16, protein 3

Breakfast Pulled Pork

Preparation time: 10 minutes
Cooking time: 10 hours
Servings: 4

Ingredients:
- 4 pounds pork butt roast
- 1 tablespoon cumin powder
- 2 tablespoons chili powder
- 1 teaspoon coriander, ground
- 1 tablespoon oregano, dried
- 2 yellow onions, sliced
- 2 avocados, peeled, pitted and sliced

Directions:
1. In your slow cooker, mix pork butt with chili, cumin, oregano and coriander and rub well.
2. Add onions, cover and cook on Low for 10 hours.
3. Shred meat using 2 forks, divide between plates, top each with avocado slices and serve for breakfast.

Enjoy!

Nutrition: calories 300, fat 4, fiber 10, carbs 24, protein 5

Sweet Potato Breakfast Mix

Preparation time: 10 minutes
Cooking time: 2 hours and 30 minutes
Servings: 2

Ingredients:

- 1 yellow bell pepper, roughly chopped
- 1 orange bell pepper, roughly chopped
- 3 ounces butternut squash, peeled and cubed
- 3 ounces sweet potatoes, peeled and cubed
- 2 tablespoons coconut oil
- 1 teaspoon thyme, dried
- 1 teaspoon garlic, minced
- 2 tomatoes, chopped
- 1 teaspoon mustard powder

Directions:

1. In your slow cooker, mix orange bell pepper with yellow one, butternut squash, sweet potatoes, oil, thyme, garlic, mustard powder and tomatoes, toss a bit, cover and cook on High for 2 hours and 30 minutes.
2. Divide between plates and serve for breakfast.

Enjoy!

Nutrition: calories 182, fat 4, fiber 7, carbs 12, protein 3

Simple Breakfast Pie

Preparation time: 10 minutes
Cooking time: 8 hours
Servings: 4

Ingredients:

- 1 sweet potato, shredded
- 8 eggs, whisked
- 2 teaspoons coconut oil, melted
- 1 pound pork sausage, crumbled
- 1 tablespoon garlic powder
- 1 yellow onion, chopped
- 2 teaspoons basil, dried
- 2 red bell peppers, chopped
- A pinch of sea salt and black pepper

Directions:

1. Grease your slow cooker with the coconut oil and add sweet potatoes.
2. Also add sausage, garlic powder, bell pepper, onion, basil, salt and pepper.
3. Add whisked eggs, toss, cover and cook on Low for 8 hours.
4. Divide between plates and serve warm.

Enjoy!

Nutrition: calories 254, fat 7, fiber 8, carbs 14, protein 6

Breakfast Sausage Casserole

Preparation time: 10 minutes
Cooking time: 4 hours
Servings: 4

Ingredients:
- 1 and 1/3 cups leek, chopped
- 2 tablespoons coconut oil, melted
- 2 teaspoons garlic, minced
- 1 cup kale, chopped
- 8 eggs, whisked
- 1 and ½ cups beef sausage, chopped
- 2/3 cup sweet potatoes, grated

Directions:
1. Heat up a pan with the oil over medium high heat, add garlic, leek and kale, stir and cook for a couple of minutes.
2. In a bowl, mix eggs with sausage and sweet potato and stir well.
3. Add sautéed veggies, stir, pour everything into your slow cooker, cover and cook on Low for 4 hours.
4. Divide this mix into plates and serve for breakfast.
Enjoy!

Nutrition: calories 232, fat 4, fiber 8, carbs 12, protein 4

Mexican Breakfast

Preparation time: 10 minutes
Cooking time: 6 hours
Servings: 5

Ingredients:
- 8 eggs, whisked
- 1 sweet potato, cubed
- 1 yellow onion, chopped
- ½ pound turkey bacon, cooked and crumbled
- 8 ounces mushrooms, chopped
- 1 red bell pepper, chopped
- Guacamole for serving
- Salsa for serving

Directions:
1. In your slow cooker, mix eggs with sweet potato, onion, bacon, mushrooms and red bell pepper, stir a bit, cover and cook on Low for 6 hours.
2. Divide between plates, top with guacamole and salsa and serve for breakfast.
Enjoy!

Nutrition: calories 213, fat 4, fiber 6, carbs 12, protein 4

Sausage and Eggs

Preparation time: 10 minutes
Cooking time: 3 hours
Servings: 6

Ingredients:
- 1 broccoli head, florets separated and chopped
- 12 ounces pork sausage, cooked and sliced
- 2 garlic cloves, minced
- 10 eggs, whisked
- A pinch of salt and black pepper

Directions:
1. In a bowl, mix eggs with salt, pepper, garlic, sausage slices and broccoli and whisk well.
2. Transfer this to your slow cooker, cover and cook on High for 3 hours.
3. Slice, divide between plates and serve.

Enjoy!

Nutrition: calories 261, fat 4, fiber 7, carbs 10, protein 3

Eggs and Bacon Casserole

Preparation time: 10 minutes
Cooking time: 8 hours
Servings: 6

Ingredients:
- 1 red onion, chopped
- 1 pound bacon, cooked and chopped
- 1 red bell pepper, chopped
- 2 garlic cloves, minced
- 1 teaspoon ghee
- 2 sweet potatoes, grated
- 12 eggs, whisked
- 1 cup coconut milk
- 1 teaspoon dill, chopped
- A pinch of red pepper, crushed
- A pinch of sea salt and black pepper

Directions:
1. In a bowl, mix eggs with onion, bacon, garlic, bell pepper, sweet potatoes, coconut milk, dill, salt, pepper and red pepper and whisk everything.
2. Grease your slow cooker with the ghee, add eggs and bacon mix, cover and cook on Low for 8 hours.
3. Slice eggs casserole, divide between plates and serve.

Enjoy!

Nutrition: calories 261, fat 6, fiber 6, carbs 12, protein 4

Delicious Sweet Potatoes and Pork Casserole

Preparation time: 10 minutes
Cooking time: 6 hours
Servings: 4

Ingredients:
- 2 red onions, chopped
- 7 eggs, whisked
- 2 sweet potatoes, grated
- 2 tablespoons smoked paprika
- 1 pound pork, ground
- 2 teaspoons coconut oil, melted

Directions:
1. In a bowl, mix eggs with onions, sweet potatoes, paprika and minced meat and whisk well.
2. Grease your slow cooker with coconut oil, add eggs and meat mix, cover and cook on Low for 6 hours.
3. Slice, divide between plates and serve warm for breakfast.

Enjoy!

Nutrition: calories 261, fat 6, fiber 4, carbs 12, protein 3

Tasty Breakfast Meatloaf

Preparation time: 10 minutes
Cooking time: 3 hours and 10 minutes
Servings: 4

Ingredients:
- 3 garlic cloves, minced
- 1 yellow onion, chopped
- 2 pounds pork, ground
- 1 tablespoon coconut oil
- ¼ cup almond flour
- 1 teaspoon red pepper flakes, crushed
- 1 teaspoon oregano, dried
- 1 tablespoon sage, chopped
- 1 teaspoon marjoram, dried
- 2 eggs
- 1 tablespoon smoked paprika

Directions:
1. Heat up a pan with the oil over medium high heat, add onion, stir and sauté for 3 minutes.
2. Add garlic, stir and cook for 3 minutes more.
3. In a bowl, mix sautéed onions and garlic with pork, almond flour, pepper flakes, oregano, sage, marjoram, paprika and eggs and stir really well.
4. Shape your meatloaf using your wet hands, put it in your slow cooker, cover and cook on Low for 3 hours.
5. Leave meatloaf to cool down, slice and serve it for breakfast.

Enjoy!

Nutrition: calories 273, fat 4, fiber 7, carbs 14, protein 5

Breakfast Salad

Preparation time: 10 minutes
Cooking time: 10 hours
Servings: 4

Ingredients:

- 1 yellow onion, chopped
- 3 pounds pork shoulder
- 1 tablespoon cumin, ground
- 2 tablespoon smoked paprika
- 1 tablespoon chili powder
- 1 tablespoon garlic powder
- 2 teaspoons oregano, dried
- 1 teaspoon allspice, ground
- 1 teaspoon cinnamon powder
- A pinch of salt and black pepper
- Juice from 1 lemon
- 1 romaine lettuce head, leaves torn

Directions:

1. In your slow cooker, mix pork with onion, cumin, paprika, chili, garlic powder, oregano, allspice, cinnamon, salt, pepper and lemon juice, rub well, cover and cook on Low for 10 hours.
2. Transfer pork shoulder to a cutting board, cool it down, shred using 2 forks and transfer to a bowl.
3. Add lettuce leaves, add some of the cooking liquid from the pot, toss and serve right away.
Enjoy!

Nutrition: calories 261, fat 4, fiber 6, carbs 13, protein 3

Delicious Veggie Omelet

Preparation time: 10 minutes
Cooking time: 2 hours
Servings: 4

Ingredients:

- ½ cup coconut milk
- 6 eggs, whisked
- A pinch of salt and black pepper
- A pinch of garlic powder
- A pinch of chili powder
- 1 red bell pepper, chopped
- 1 cup cauliflower florets
- 1 garlic clove, minced
- 1 yellow onion, chopped
- 2 tomatoes, chopped
- 1 tablespoon parsley, chopped
- Cooking spray

Directions:

1. In a bowl, mix eggs with coconut milk, salt, pepper, garlic powder, chili powder, bell pepper, cauliflower, garlic and onion and whisk well.
2. Grease your slow cooker with cooking spray, add eggs mix, spread, cover and cook on High for 2 hours.
3. Slice omelet, divide between plates and serve with chopped tomatoes and parsley on top.
Enjoy!

Nutrition: calories 142, fat 3, fiber 4, carbs 7, protein 4

Chorizo Breakfast Casserole

Preparation time: 10 minutes
Cooking time: 10 hours
Servings: 8

Ingredients:
- 1 pound chorizo, casings removed and chopped
- 12 eggs, whisked
- 1 yellow onion, chopped
- 1 cup coconut milk
- 1 butternut squash, peeled and cubed
- 1 teaspoon ghee

Directions:
1. Heat up a pan over medium high heat, add chorizo, stir and cook for a few minutes.
2. Add onion, stir, cook for a couple more minutes and take off heat.
3. In a bowl, mix eggs with chorizo, onion, coconut milk and squash and whisk.
4. Grease your slow cooker with the ghee, pour eggs and chorizo mix, cover and cook on Low for 10 hours.
5. Slice chorizo casserole, divide between plates and serve for breakfast.

Enjoy!

Nutrition: calories 246, fat 4, fiber 6, carbs 8, protein 5

Eggs and Sweet Potato Pesto

Preparation time: 10 minutes
Cooking time: 4 hours
Servings: 4

Ingredients:
- 4 sweet potatoes, pricked with a fork
- 4 eggs, fried
- 2/3 cup walnuts, soaked for 12 hours and drained
- 1 garlic clove
- 1 and ½ cups basil leaves
- ½ cup olive oil
- Juice from ½ lemon
- A pinch of salt and black pepper

Directions:
1. Wrap sweet potatoes in tin foil, add them to your slow cooker, cover and cook on High for 4hours.
2. Transfer sweet potatoes to a cutting board, unwrap, cool them down, peel and mash them with a fork.
3. In your food processor, mix walnuts with garlic, basil, oil, salt, pepper and lemon juice and pulse really well.
4. Mix sweet potato mash with basil pesto and stir well.
5. Divide fried eggs between plates, top each with sweet potato pesto and serve for breakfast.

Enjoy!

Nutrition: calories 163, fat 5, fiber 6, carbs 13, protein 4

Delicious Pumpkin Butter

Preparation time: 10 minutes
Cooking time: 4 hours
Servings: 8

Ingredients:
- 30 ounces pumpkin puree
- ½ cup apple cider
- 1 cup coconut sugar
- 1 teaspoon vanilla extract
- 1 teaspoon cinnamon, ground
- 1 teaspoon nutmeg, ground
- 2 teaspoon lemon juice
- 1 teaspoon ginger, grated
- ¼ teaspoon cloves, ground
- ¼ teaspoon allspice, ground

Directions:
1. In your slow cooker, mix pumpkin puree with apple cider, coconut sugar, vanilla extract, cinnamon, nutmeg, lemon juice, ginger, cloves and allspice, stir, cover and cook on Low for 4 hours.
2. Blend using an immersion blender, cool down and serve for breakfast.

Enjoy!

Nutrition: calories 222, fat 3, fiber 3, carbs 6, protein 3

Delicious Carrot Breakfast

Preparation time: 10 minutes
Cooking time: 6 hours
Servings: 10

Ingredients:
- 1 cup raisins
- 6 cups water
- 23 ounces applesauce, unsweetened
- 1/3 cup splenda
- 2 tablespoons cinnamon powder
- 14 ounces carrots, shredded
- 8 ounces canned pineapple, crushed
- 1 tablespoon pumpkin pie spice

Directions:
1. In your slow cooker, mix carrots with applesauce, raisins, splenda, cinnamon, pineapple and pumpkin pie spice, stir, cover and cook on Low for 6 hours.
2. Divide into bowls and serve for breakfast.

Enjoy!

Nutrition: calories 139, fat 2, fiber 3, carbs 20, protein 4

Paleo Slow Cooker Side Dish Recipes

Summer Veggies Surprise

Preparation time: 10 minutes
Cooking time: 3 hours
Servings: 4

Ingredients:

- 1 and ½ cups red onion, cut into medium chunks
- 1 cup cherry tomatoes, halved
- 2 cups okra, sliced
- 2 and ½ cups zucchini, sliced
- 2 cups yellow bell pepper, chopped
- 1 cup mushrooms, sliced
- 2 tablespoons basil, chopped
- 1 tablespoon thyme, chopped
- ½ cup olive oil
- ½ cup balsamic vinegar

Directions:

1. In a large bowl, mix onion chunks with tomatoes, okra, zucchini, bell pepper, mushrooms, basil and thyme.
2. Add oil and vinegar and toss to coat everything.
3. Transfer to your slow cooker, cover and cook on High for 3 hours.
4. Divide between plates and serve as a side dish.

Enjoy!

Nutrition: calories 150, fat 2, fiber 2, carbs 6, protein 5

Sweet Cabbage

Preparation time: 10 minutes
Cooking time: 6 hours
Servings: 4

Ingredients:

- 1 onion, sliced
- 1 cabbage, shredded
- 2 apples, peeled, cored and roughly chopped
- A pinch of sea salt
- Black pepper to the taste
- 1 cup apple juice
- ½ cup chicken stock
- 3 tablespoons mustard
- 1 tablespoon coconut oil

Directions:

1. Grease your slow cooker with the coconut oil and place apples, cabbage and onions inside.
2. In a bowl, mix stock with mustard, a pinch of salt, black pepper and the apple juice and whisk well.
3. Pour this over into the slow cooker as well, cover and cook on Low for 6 hours.
4. Divide between plates and serve right away as a side dish.

Enjoy!

Nutrition: calories 200, fat 4, fiber 2, carbs 8, protein 6

Delicious Sweet Potatoes and Bacon

Preparation time: 10 minutes
Cooking time: 3 hours
Servings: 4

Ingredients:

- ½ cup orange juice
- 4 pounds sweet potatoes, sliced
- 3 tablespoons agave nectar
- ½ teaspoon thyme, dried
- ½ teaspoon sage, crushed
- A pinch of sea salt
- 2 tablespoons olive oil
- 4 bacon slices, cooked and crumbled

Directions:

1. In your slow cooker mix sweet potato slices with orange juice, agave nectar, thyme, sage, sea salt, olive oil and bacon, cover and cook on High for 3 hours.
2. Divide between plates and serve as a tasty side dish!

Enjoy!

Nutrition: calories 189, fat 4, fiber 4, carbs 9, protein 5

Delicious Glazed Carrots

Preparation time: 10 minutes
Cooking time: 3 hours
Servings: 8

Ingredients:

- 2 pounds carrots, sliced
- ½ cup water
- ½ cup raw honey
- A pinch of sea salt
- ½ teaspoon cinnamon, ground
- A pinch of nutmeg, ground

Directions:

1. Put carrots in your slow cooker.
2. Add water, raw honey, salt, cinnamon and nutmeg, toss well, cover and cook on High for 3 hours.
3. Stir again, divide between plates and serve as a side dish.

Enjoy!

Nutrition: calories 170, fat 3, fiber 4, carbs 7, protein 3

Garlic Mushrooms

Preparation time: 10 minutes
Cooking time: 4 hours
Servings: 4

Ingredients:

- 2 bay leaves
- 4 garlic cloves, minced
- 24 ounces mushroom caps
- ¼ teaspoon thyme dried
- ½ teaspoon basil, dried
- ½ teaspoon oregano, dried
- 1 cup veggie stock
- Black pepper to the taste
- 2 tablespoons olive oil
- 2 tablespoons parsley, chopped

Directions:

1. Grease your slow cooker with the olive oil.
2. Add mushrooms, garlic, bay leaves, thyme, basil, oregano, black pepper and stock.
3. Cover and cook on Low for 4 hours.
4. Divide between plates and serve with parsley sprinkled on top.

Enjoy!

Nutrition: calories 122, fat 6, fiber 1, carbs 8, protein 5

Delicious Brussels Sprouts

Preparation time: 10 minutes
Cooking time: 3 hours
Servings: 4

Ingredients:

- 1 cup red onion, sliced
- 2 pounds Brussels sprouts, halved
- A pinch of sea salt
- Black pepper to the taste
- 2 tablespoons olive oil
- ¼ cup apple cider
- ¼ cup maple syrup
- 1 tablespoon thyme, chopped

Directions:

1. Put the oil in your slow cooker.
2. Add Brussels sprouts, a pinch of salt, black pepper to the taste, onion, cider, maple syrup and thyme.
3. Toss everything to coat, cover and cook on High for 3 hours.
4. Divide between plates and serve warm.

Enjoy!

Nutrition: calories 100, fat 4, fiber 2, carbs 10, protein 3

Delicious Beets and Carrots

Preparation time: 10 minutes
Cooking time: 6 hours
Servings: 4

Ingredients:

- ¾ cup pomegranate juice
- A pinch of sea salt
- 2 tablespoons agave nectar
- 2 teaspoons ginger, grated
- 3 pounds red beets, peeled and cut into wedges
- 4 carrots, peeled and sliced

Directions:

1. Put pomegranate juice in a pot and heat up over medium heat.
2. Add a pinch of salt and the agave nectar, stir and cook for 2 minutes.
3. Put beets and carrots in your slow cooker and ginger and stir gently.
4. Add pomegranate juice, toss a bit, cover and cook on Low for 6 hours.
5. Divide beets and carrots between plates and serve warm or cold.

Enjoy!

Nutrition: calories 100, fat 1, fiber 2, carbs 5, protein 3

Special Acorn Squash and Cranberry Sauce

Preparation time: 10 minutes
Cooking time: 7 hours
Servings: 4

Ingredients:

¼-cup raisins
2 acorn squash, peeled and cut into medium wedges
16 ounces canned cranberry sauce, unsweetened
¼ teaspoon cinnamon, ground
A pinch of sea salt
Black pepper to the taste

Directions:

1. Place acorn pieces in your slow cooker, add cranberry sauce, raisins, cinnamon, salt and pepper, stir, cover and cook on Low for 7 hours.
2. Divide between plates and serve hot as a Paleo side.

Enjoy!

Nutrition: calories 230, fat 3, fiber 3, carbs 10, protein 2

Crazy Eggplant Delight

Preparation time: 10 minutes
Cooking time: 6 hours
Servings: 4

Ingredients:

- 1 eggplant, roughly chopped
- 1 tablespoon olive oil
- 2 garlic cloves, minced
- 2 carrots, chopped
- 1 yellow onion, chopped
- 10 ounces canned tomatoes, roughly chopped
- 1 tablespoon ras all hanout
- A pinch of cayenne pepper
- 1 teaspoon cumin, ground
- A handful cilantro, chopped

Directions:

1. Put the oil in your slow cooker.
2. Add eggplant, garlic, carrots, onion, tomatoes, cumin, ras eh hanout and cayenne.
3. Toss everything, cover and cook on Low for 6 hours.
   Sprinkle cilantro on top, divide between plates and serve with a tasty pork steak.

Enjoy!

Nutrition: calories 120, fat 4, fiber 2, carbs 10, protein 3

Tasty Zucchini

Preparation time: 10 minutes
Cooking time: 6 hours
Servings: 6

Ingredients:

- 2 cups zucchinis, sliced
- 1 teaspoon Italian seasoning
- Black pepper to the taste
- 2 cups yellow squash, peeled and cut into wedges
- 1 teaspoon garlic powder
- 2 tablespoons olive oil
- A pinch of sea salt
- ¼ cup pork rinds, crushed

Directions:

1. Put the oil in your slow cooker.
2. Add zucchini and squash pieces, Italian seasoning, black pepper, salt and garlic powder, toss well, cover and cook on Low for 6 hours.
3. Divide between plates and serve with pork rind sprinkled on top.

Enjoy!

Nutrition: calories 100, fat 2, fiber 4, carbs 8, protein 5

Scalloped Sweet Potatoes

Preparation time: 10 minutes
Cooking time: 4 hours
Servings: 12

Ingredients:
- 2 pounds sweet potatoes, peeled and cubed
- 10 ounces coconut cream
- 1 and ½ cups coconut milk
- ½ cup ghee, melted+ 1 teaspoon
- ¼ cup yellow onion, chopped
- A pinch of salt and black pepper

Directions:
1. In a bowl, mix sweet potato cubes with coconut cream, coconut milk, ghee, onion, salt and pepper, stir well, and pour in your slow cooker after you've greased it with 1 teaspoon ghee, cover Crockpot and cook on Low for 4 hours.
2. Leave scalloped potatoes aside to cool down, slice, divide between plates and serve as a side dish.

Enjoy!

Nutrition: calories 234, fat 12, fiber 1, carbs 20, protein 6

Broccoli Side Dish

Preparation time: 10 minutes
Cooking time: 3 hours
Servings: 10

Ingredients:
- 6 cups broccoli florets, chopped
- 10 ounces coconut cream
- ¼ cup yellow onion, chopped
- 1 and ½ cups cashew cheese, shredded
- 2 tablespoons ghee

Directions:
1. Add ghee to your slow cooker, add broccoli florets, onion and coconut cream and toss.
2. Sprinkle cashew cheese on top, cover and cook on High for 3 hours.
3. Divide between plates and serve as a side dish.

Enjoy!

Nutrition: calories 158, fat 11, fiber 3, carbs 11, protein 5

Green Beans

Preparation time: 10 minutes
Cooking time: 2 hours
Servings: 12

Ingredients:
- 16 cups green beans, halved
- ½ cup ghee, melted
- ½ cup coconut sugar
- ¾ teaspoon coconut aminos
- A pinch of salt and black pepper

Directions:
1. In your slow cooker, mix green beans with coconut sugar, aminos, salt, pepper and melted ghee, toss well, cover and cook on Low for 3 hours.
2. Divide between plates and serve as a side dish.

Enjoy!

Nutrition: calories 160, fat 4, fiber 5, carbs 12, protein 3

Cauliflower Pilaf

Preparation time: 10 minutes
Cooking time: 3 hours
Servings: 6

Ingredients:
- 1 cup cauliflower rice
- 6 green onions, chopped
- 3 tablespoons ghee, melted
- 2 garlic cloves, minced
- ½ pound Portobello mushrooms, sliced
- 2 cups warm water
- A pinch of salt and black pepper

Directions:
1. In your slow cooker, mix cauliflower rice with green onions, melted ghee, garlic, mushrooms, water, salt and pepper, stir well, cover and cook on Low for 3 hours.
2. Divide between plates and serve as a side dish.

Enjoy!

Nutrition: calories 200, fat 5, fiber 3, carbs 14, protein 4

Butternut Squash Side Dish

Preparation time: 10 minutes
Cooking time: 4 hours
Servings: 8

Ingredients:
- 1 tablespoon olive oil
- 1 cup carrots, chopped
- 1 yellow onion, chopped
- 1 teaspoon stevia
- 1 and ½ teaspoons curry powder
- 1 garlic clove, minced
- 1 big butternut squash, peeled and cubed
- A pinch of sea salt and black pepper
- ¼ teaspoon ginger, grated
- ½ teaspoon cinnamon powder
- 3 cups coconut milk

Directions:
1. Add the oil to your slow cooker and spread on the bottom.
2. Add carrots, onion, stevia, curry powder, garlic, squash, salt, pepper, ginger, cinnamon and coconut milk, stir well, cover and cook on Low for 4 hours.
3. Stir, divide between plates and serve as a side dish.

Enjoy!

Nutrition: calories 200, fat 4, fiber 4, carbs 17, protein 4

Sausage Side Dish

Preparation time: 10 minutes
Cooking time: 2 hours and 30 minutes
Servings: 12

Ingredients:
- ½ cup ghee, melted
- 1 pound pork sausage, ground
- ½ pound mushrooms, sliced
- 6 celery ribs, chopped
- 2 yellow onions, chopped
- 2 garlic cloves, minced
- 1 tablespoon sage, chopped
- 1 cup cranberries, dried
- ½ cup cauliflower florets, chopped
- ½ cup veggie stock

Directions:
1. Heat up a pan with the ghee over medium high heat, add sausage, stir and cook for a couple of minutes.
2. Transfer this to your slow cooker, add mushrooms, celery, onion, garlic, sage, cranberries, cauliflower and stock, stir, cover and cook on High for 2 hours and 30 minutes.
3. Divide between plates and serve as a side dish.

Enjoy!

Nutrition: calories 200, fat 3, fiber 6, carbs 9, protein 4

Sweet Potatoes and Parsley

Preparation time: 10 minutes
Cooking time: 6 hours
Servings: 8

Ingredients:

- 2 pounds sweet potatoes, cut into medium pieces
- 1 carrot, chopped
- 1 celery rib, chopped
- ¼ cup yellow onion, chopped
- 2 cups veggie stock
- 1 tablespoon parsley, chopped
- 2 tablespoons ghee, melted
- 1 garlic clove, minced
- A pinch of salt and black pepper

Directions:

1. In your slow cooker, mix sweet potatoes with carrot, celery, onion, garlic, salt, pepper and stock, stir, cover and cook on Low for 6 hours.
2. Transfer this to a bowl, add melted ghee and parsley, stir, divide between plates and serve as a side dish.

Enjoy!

Nutrition: calories 114, fat 3, fiber 4, carbs 18, protein 3

Glazed Carrots

Preparation time: 10 minutes
Cooking time: 6 hours
Servings: 6

Ingredients:

- ½ cup peach preserves
- ½ cup ghee, melted
- 2 pounds baby carrots
- 2 tablespoon stevia
- 1 teaspoon vanilla extract
- A pinch of salt and black pepper
- A pinch of nutmeg, ground
- ½ teaspoon cinnamon powder
- 2 tablespoons water

Directions:

1. Put baby carrots in your slow cooker, add melted ghee, peach preserves, stevia, vanilla, salt, pepper, nutmeg, cinnamon and water, toss well, cover and cook on Low for 6 hours.
2. Divide between plates and serve as a side dish.

Enjoy!

Nutrition: calories 283, fat 14, fiber 4, carbs 28, protein 3

Sweet Potatoes Side Salad

Preparation time: 10 minutes
Cooking time: 7 hours
Servings: 10

Ingredients:
- 6 bacon strips, chopped
- 2 pounds sweet potatoes, cubed
- 7 ounces cashew cheese, shredded
- 10 ounces coconut cream
- ½ cup almond milk
- 3 tablespoons red onion, chopped
- 1 tablespoon garlic, minced
- 1 tablespoon thyme, chopped
- A pinch of salt and black pepper

Directions:
1. In your slow cooker, mix bacon with sweet potato cubes, cashew cheese, coconut cream, almond milk, onion, garlic, thyme, salt and pepper, stir, cover and cook on Low for 7 hours.
2. Divide on plates and serve as a side salad.

Enjoy!

Nutrition: calories 230, fat 12, fiber 3, carbs 20, protein 6

Fresh Butternut Squash Side Salad

Preparation time: 10 minutes
Cooking time: 4 hours
Servings: 12

Ingredients:
- 3 pounds butternut squash, peeled and cubed
- 1 yellow onion, chopped
- 2 teaspoons thyme, chopped
- 3 garlic cloves, minced
- A pinch of salt and black pepper
- 10 ounces veggie stock
- 6 ounces baby spinach

Directions:
1. In your slow cooker, mix squash cubes with onion, thyme, salt, pepper and stock, stir, cover and cook on Low for 4 hours.
2. Transfer squash mix to a bowl, add spinach, more salt and pepper if you want, toss, divide between plates and serve as a side dish.

Enjoy!

Nutrition: calories 100, fat 1, fiber 4, carbs 18, protein 4

Rich Mushrooms Mix

Preparation time: 10 minutes
Cooking time: 4 hours
Servings: 6

Ingredients:
- 1 yellow onion, chopped
- 1 pounds mushrooms, halved
- ½ cup ghee, melted
- 1 teaspoon Italian seasoning
- A pinch of salt and black pepper
- 1 teaspoon sweet paprika

Directions:
1. In your slow cooker, mix mushrooms with onion, ghee, Italian seasoning, salt, pepper and paprika, toss, cover and cook on Low for 4 hours.
2. Divide between plates and serve as a side dish.

Enjoy!

Nutrition: calories 100, fat 6, fiber 1, carbs 8, protein 4

Cauliflower Rice and Spinach

Preparation time: 10 minutes
Cooking time: 3 hours
Servings: 8

Ingredients:
- 2 garlic cloves, minced
- 2 tablespoons ghee, melted
- 1 yellow onion, chopped
- ¼ teaspoon thyme, dried
- 3 cups veggie stock
- 20 ounces spinach, chopped
- 6 ounces coconut cream
- A pinch of salt and black pepper
- 2 cups cauliflower rice

Directions:
1. Heat up a pan with the ghee over medium heat, add onion, stir and cook for 4 minutes.
2. Add garlic and thyme, stir and cook for 1 minute more.
3. Add stock, stir, bring to a simmer and take off heat.
4. Add spinach, coconut cream, salt and pepper, stir and transfer everything to your slow cooker.
5. Add cauliflower rice as well, stir a bit, cover and cook on High for 3 hours.
6. Divide between plates and serve as a side dish.

Enjoy!

Nutrition: calories 200, fat 4, fiber 4, carbs 8, protein 2

Maple Sweet Potatoes Side Dish

Preparation time: 10 minutes
Cooking time: 5 hours
Servings: 10

Ingredients:
- 8 sweet potatoes, halved and sliced
- 1 cup walnuts, chopped
- ½ cup cherries, dried and chopped
- ½ cup maple syrup
- ¼ cup apple juice
- A pinch of salt

Directions:
1. Arrange sweet potatoes in your slow cooker, add walnuts, dried cherries, maple syrup, apple juice and a pinch of salt, toss a bit, cover and cook on Low for 5 hours.
2. Divide between plates and serve as a side dish.

Enjoy!

Nutrition: calories 271, fat 6, fiber 4, carbs 26, protein 6

Creamy Spinach

Preparation time: 10 minutes
Cooking time: 5 hours
Servings: 6

Ingredients:
- 20 ounces spinach
- 2 cups coconut cream
- 1 cup cashew cheese, shredded
- ¼ cup ghee, melted

Directions:
1. In your slow cooker, mix spinach with coconut cream and ghee and toss well.
2. Add cashew cheese, cover and cook on Low for 5 hours.
3. Divide between plates and serve as a side dish.

Enjoy!

Nutrition: calories 230, fat 12, fiber 2, carbs 9, protein 12

Chipotle Shredded Sweet Potatoes

Preparation time: 10 minutes
Cooking time: 4 hours
Servings: 10

Ingredients:
- 1 sweet onion, chopped
- 2 tablespoons olive oil
- ¼ cup parsley, chopped
- 2 shallots, chopped
- 2 teaspoons chipotle pepper, crushed
- A pinch of salt and black pepper
- 4 big sweet potatoes, shredded
- 8 ounces coconut cream
- 16 ounces bacon, cooked and chopped
- ½ teaspoon sweet paprika
- Cooking spray

Directions:
1. Heat up a pan with the oil over medium high heat, add shallots and onion, stir, cook for 6 minutes and transfer to a bowl.
2. Add parsley, chipotle pepper, salt, pepper, sweet potatoes, coconut cream, paprika and bacon, stir and pour everything in your slow cooker after you've greased it with some cooking spray.
3. Cover, cook on Low for 4 hours, leave aside to cool down a bit, slice, divide between plates and serve as a side dish.

Enjoy!

Nutrition: calories 260, fat 14, fiber 6, carbs 20, protein 15

Kale Side Dish

Preparation time: 10 minutes
Cooking time: 6 hours
Servings: 6

Ingredients:
- 8 ounces ham hock slices
- 1 and ½ cups water
- 1 cup chicken stock
- 12 cups kale leaves, torn
- A pinch of salt and cayenne pepper
- 2 tablespoons olive oil
- 1 yellow onion, chopped
- 2 tablespoons apple cider vinegar
- Cooking spray

Directions:
1. Put ham in a heat proof bowl, add the water and the stock, cover and microwave for 3 minutes.
2. Heat up a pan with the oil over medium high heat, add onion, stir and cook for 5 minutes.
3. Drain ham and add it to your slow cooker, add sautéed onions, kale, salt, cayenne and vinegar, toss, cover and cook on Low for 6 hours.
4. Divide between plates and serve as a side dish.

Enjoy!

Nutrition: calories 200, fat 4, fiber 7, carbs 10, protein 3

Sweet Potato Mash

Preparation time: 10 minutes
Cooking time: 5 hours
Servings: 6

Ingredients:
- 2 pounds sweet potatoes, peeled and sliced
- 1 tablespoon cinnamon powder
- 1 cup apple juice
- 1 teaspoon nutmeg, ground
- ¼ teaspoon cloves, ground
- ½ teaspoon allspice
- 1 tablespoon ghee, melted

Directions:
1. In your slow cooker, mix sweet potatoes with cinnamon, apple juice, nutmeg, cloves and allspice, stir, cover and cook on Low for 5 hours.
2. Mash using a potato masher, add ghee, whisk well, divide between plates and serve as a side dish.

Enjoy!

Nutrition: calories 111, fat 2, fiber 2, carbs 16, protein 3

Incredible Veggie Mix

Preparation time: 10 minutes
Cooking time: 3 hours
Servings: 4

Ingredients:
- 2 red bell peppers, roughly chopped
- 1 sweet potato, peeled and cubed
- ½ cup garlic cloves
- 3 zucchinis, sliced
- 2 tablespoons olive oil
- 1 teaspoon Italian seasoning
- A pinch of salt and black pepper

Directions:
1. In your slow cooker, mix red bell peppers with sweet potato, garlic, zucchinis, oil, salt, pepper and Italian seasoning, toss, cover and cook on High for 3 hours.
2. Divide between plates and serve as a side dish.

Enjoy!

Nutrition: calories 120, fat 3, fiber 4, carbs 6, protein 3

Cauliflower Mash

Preparation time: 10 minutes
Cooking time: 5 hours
Servings: 6

Ingredients:

- 1 cauliflower head, florets separated
- 1/3 cup dill, chopped
- 6 garlic cloves
- 2 tablespoons ghee, melted
- A pinch of salt and black pepper

Directions:

1. Put cauliflower in your slow cooker, add dill, garlic and water to cover cauliflower, cover and cook on High for 5 hours.
2. Drain cauliflower and dill, add salt, pepper and ghee, mash using a potato masher, whisk well and serve as a side dish.

Enjoy!

Nutrition: calories 187, fat 4, fiber 5, carbs 7, protein 3

Sweet Potatoes with Orange and Sage

Preparation time: 10 minutes
Cooking time: 6 hours
Servings: 10

Ingredients:

- 4 pounds sweet potatoes, peeled and cut into medium slices
- ½ cup orange juice
- 2 tablespoons coconut sugar
- A pinch of salt and black pepper
- 1 teaspoon sage, dried
- ½ teaspoon thyme, dried
- 2 tablespoons ghee, melted
- 4 bacon slices, cooked and crumbled

Directions:

1. Place sweet potatoes in your slow cooker.
2. In a bowl, mix orange juice with coconut sugar, salt, pepper, sage, thyme and ghee and whisk really well.
3. Add this over sweet potatoes, also add bacon, cover and cook on Low for 6 hours.
4. Divide between plates and serve as a side dish.

Enjoy!

Nutrition: calories 189, fat 4, fiber 4, carbs 29, protein 4

Paleo Slow Cooker Snack and Appetizer Recipes

Simple Meatballs

Preparation time: 10 minutes
Cooking time: 8 hours
Servings: 4

Ingredients:

- 1 and ½ pounds beef, ground
- 1 egg, whisked
- 16 ounces canned tomatoes, crushed
- 14 ounces canned tomato puree
- ¼ cup parsley, chopped
- 2 garlic cloves, minced
- 1 yellow onion, chopped
- Black pepper to the taste

Directions:

1. In a bowl, mix beef with egg, parsley, garlic, black pepper and onion and stir well.
2. Shape 16 meatballs, place them in your slow cooker, add tomato puree and crushed tomatoes on top, cover and cook on Low for 8 hours.
3. Arrange them on a platter and serve.

Enjoy!

Nutrition: calories 160, fat 5, fiber 3, carbs 10, protein 7

Tasty Chicken Wings

Preparation time: 10 minutes
Cooking time: 3 hours
Servings: 6

Ingredients:

- 2 tablespoons garlic, minced
- 2 and ¼ cups pineapple juice
- 3 tablespoons coconut aminos
- 2 tablespoons tapioca flour
- 1 tablespoon ginger, minced
- 1 teaspoon sesame oil
- A pinch of sea salt
- 3 pounds chicken wings
- A pinch of red pepper flakes, crushed
- 2 tablespoons 5 spice powder
- Sesame seeds, toasted for serving
- Chopped cilantro, for serving

Directions:

1. Put 2 cups pineapple juice in your slow cooker, add sesame oil, a pinch of salt, coconut aminos, ginger and garlic and whisk well.
2. In a bowl, mix tapioca flour with the rest of the pineapple juice, whisk and also add to your slow cooker.
3. Whisk everything and then add chicken wings.
4. Season them with pepper flakes and 5 spice, toss everything, cover and cook on High for 3 hours.
5. Transfer chicken wings to a platter and sprinkle cilantro and sesame seeds on top.
6. Transfer sauce from the slow cooker to a pot and heat it up for 2 minutes over medium high heat.
7. Whisk well, pour into small bowls and serve your wings with it.

Enjoy!

Nutrition: calories 200, fat 4, fiber 4, carbs 9, protein 20

Simple Jalapeno Poppers

Preparation time: 10 minutes
Cooking time: 3 hours
Servings: 4

Ingredients:

- ½ pound chorizo, chopped
- 10 jalapenos, tops cut off and deseeded
- 1 small white onion, chopped
- ½ pound beef, ground
- ¼ teaspoon garlic powder
- 1 tablespoon maple syrup
- 1 tablespoon mustard
- 1/3 cup water

Directions:

1. IN a bowl, mix beef with chorizo, garlic powder and onion and stir.
2. Stuff your jalapenos with the mix and place them in your slow cooker.
3. Add the water, cover and cook on High for 3 hours.
4. Transfer jalapeno poppers to a lined baking sheet.
5. IN a bowl, mix maple syrup with mustard and whisk well.
6. Brush poppers with this mix, introduce in preheated broiler and cook for 10 minutes.
7. Arrange on a platter and serve.

Enjoy!

Nutrition: calories 200, fat 2, fiber 3, carbs 8, protein 3

Tasty Fish Sticks

Preparation time: 10 minutes
Cooking time: 2 hours
Servings: 4

Ingredients:

- 2 eggs, whisked
- 1 pound cod fillets, cut into medium strips
- 1 and ½ cups almond flour
- A pinch of sea salt
- Black pepper to the taste
- ½ cup tapioca flour
- ¼ teaspoon paprika
- Cooking spray

Directions:

1. In a bowl, mix almond flour, salt, pepper, tapioca and paprika and stir.
2. Put the eggs in another bowl.
3. Dip fish sticks in the eggs and then dredge in flour mix.
4. Spray your slow cooker with cooking spray and arrange fish sticks in it.
5. Cover and cook on High for 2 hours.
6. Arrange on a platter and serve.

Enjoy!

Nutrition: calories 200, fat 2, fiber 4, carbs 7, protein 12

Spicy Pecans

Preparation time: 10 minutes
Cooking time: 2 hours and 15 minutes
Servings: 5

Ingredients:
- 1 pound pecans, halved
- 2 tablespoons olive oil
- 1 teaspoon basil, dried
- 1 tablespoon chili powder
- 1 teaspoon oregano, dried
- ¼ teaspoon garlic powder
- 1 teaspoon thyme, dried
- ½ teaspoon onion powder
- A pinch of cayenne pepper

Directions:
1. In your slow cooker, mix pecans with oil, basil, chili powder, oregano, garlic powder, onion powder, thyme and cayenne and toss to coat.
2. Cover and cook on High for 15 minutes.
3. Switch slow cooker to Low and cook for 2 hours.
4. Divide into bowls and serve as a snack.

Enjoy!

Nutrition: calories 78, fat 3, fiber 2, carbs 9, protein 2

Tasty Sausage Appetizer

Preparation time: 10 minutes
Cooking time: 2 hours
Servings: 15

Ingredients:
- 2 pounds sausages, sliced
- 18 ounces unsweetened Paleo apple jelly
- 9 ounces Dijon mustard

Directions:
1. Place sausage slices in your slow cooker, add apple jelly and mustard and toss to coat really well.
2. Cover and cook on Low for 2 hours stirring every 20 minutes.
3. Arrange sausage slices on a platter and serve as a Paleo appetizer.

Enjoy!

Nutrition: calories 140, fat 3, fiber 1, carbs 9, protein 10

Mini Sausages Delight

Preparation time: 10 minutes
Cooking time: 4 hours
Servings: 24

Ingredients:
- 1 pound mini sausages, smoked
- 12 ounces Paleo chili sauce
- 1 cup Paleo grape jelly

Directions:
1. Put mini sausages in your slow cooker.
2. In a bowl, mix chili sauce with grape jelly and whisk really well.
3. Add this to your slow cooker, toss sausages to coat and cook on Low for 4 hours.
4. Serve them on a platter.

Enjoy!

Nutrition: calories 200, fat 2, fiber 3, carbs 6, protein 12

Amazing Eggplant Dip

Preparation time: 10 minutes
Cooking time: 4 hours and 10 minutes
Servings: 4

Ingredients:
- 1 eggplant
- 1 zucchini, chopped
- 2 tablespoons olive oil
- 2 tablespoons balsamic vinegar
- 1 tablespoon parsley, chopped
- 1 yellow onion, chopped
- 1 celery stick, chopped
- 1 tomato, chopped
- 2 tablespoons tomato paste
- 1 and ½ teaspoons garlic, minced
- A pinch of sea salt
- Black pepper to the taste

Directions:
1. Brush eggplant with half of the oil, place on preheated grill and cook over medium high heat for 5 minutes on each side.
2. Leave aside to cool down and then chop it.
3. Grease your slow cooker with the rest of the oil and add eggplant pieces.
4. Also add, zucchini, vinegar, onion, celery, tomato, parsley, tomato paste, garlic, salt and pepper and stir everything.
5. Cover and cook on High for 4 hours.
6. Stir your spread again very well, divide into bowls and serve.

Enjoy!

Nutrition: 110, fat 1, fiber 2, carbs 7, protein 5

Incredible Spinach Dip

Preparation time: 10 minutes
Cooking time: 2 hours
Servings: 4

Ingredients:

- 1 cup almond milk
- 1 cup cashews, soaked for 2 hours and drained
- 2 tablespoons lemon juice
- 2 garlic cloves, chopped
- 2 teaspoons mustard
- 28 ounces canned artichokes, drained and chopped
- 8 ounces spinach
- 8 ounces canned water chestnuts, drained
- Black pepper to the taste
- Avocado mayonnaise

Directions:

1. In your food processor, mix cashews with garlic, almond milk, mustard and lemon juice and blend well.
2. Transfer this to your slow cooker, add chestnuts, spinach, black pepper and artichokes.
3. Stir, cover and cook on High for 2 hours.
4. Leave your dip to cool down, add avocado mayo, stir well, divide into bowls and serve.

Enjoy!

Nutrition: calories 200, fat 4, fiber 2, carbs 8, protein 5

Coconut Meatballs

Preparation time: 10 minutes
Cooking time: 4 hours
Servings: 4

Ingredients:

- 1 and ½ pounds beef
- 2 small yellow onions, chopped
- 1 egg
- A pinch of sea salt
- Black pepper to the taste
- 3 tablespoons cilantro, chopped
- 14 ounces canned coconut milk
- 2 tablespoons hot sauce
- 1 teaspoon basil, dried
- 1 tablespoon green curry paste
- 1 tablespoon coconut aminos

Directions:

1. Put the meat in a bowl, add 1 small onion, egg, salt, pepper and 1 tablespoon cilantro, stir well, shape medium-sized meatballs and place them in your slow cooker.
2. Add hot sauce, aminos, coconut milk, curry paste and basil, toss to cover all meatballs and cook on Low for 4 hours.
3. Arrange meatballs on a platter and serve with the sauce drizzled all over.

Enjoy!

Nutrition: calories 200, fat 6, fiber 2, carbs 8, protein 4

Delicious Chicken Meatballs

Preparation time: 10 minutes
Cooking time: 7 hours
Servings: 8

Ingredients:

- 46 ounces canned tomatoes, crushed
- 1 yellow onion, halved
- 5 garlic cloves, minced
- 2 tablespoons tomato paste
- 2 tablespoons olive oil
- 1 bay leaf
- 1 basil spring, chopped
- ¼ teaspoon red pepper flakes, crushed

For the meatballs:

- 1 pound chicken, ground
- 1/3 cup almond milk
- 1 egg
- 1/3 cup cashew cheese, shredded
- 1 teaspoon oregano, dried
- 2 tablespoons parsley, chopped
- A pinch of salt and black pepper

Directions:

1. In your slow cooker, mix canned tomatoes with onion, garlic, tomato paste, olive oil, bay leaf, basil and pepper flakes, stir, cover and cook on Low for 6 hours.
2. In a bowl, mix chicken meat with almond milk, egg, cashews cheese, oregano, parsley, salt and pepper, stir well and shape medium meatballs out of this mix.
3. Add meatballs to your slow cooker and cook everything on High for 1 more hour.
4. Arrange meatballs on a platter, drizzle sauce all over and serve as an appetizer.

Enjoy!

Nutrition: calories 231, fat 4, fiber 5, carbs 8, protein 2

Candied Pecans

Preparation time: 10 minutes
Cooking time: 3 hours
Servings: 4

Ingredients:

- 1 cup coconut sugar
- 1 and ½ tablespoon cinnamon powder
- 1 egg white
- 2 teaspoons vanilla extract
- 4 cups pecans
- ¼ cup water
- Cooking spray

Directions:

1. In a bowl, mix coconut sugar with cinnamon and stir.
2. In another bowl, mix egg white with vanilla and whisk well.
3. Grease your slow cooker with cooking spray and add pecans.
4. Add egg white mix and toss.
5. Add coconut sugar mix, toss again, cover and cook on Low for 3 hours.
6. Divide pecans into bowls and serve as a snack.

Enjoy!

Nutrition: calories 172, fat 3, fiber 5, carbs 8, protein 2

Peanuts Snack

Preparation time: 10 minutes
Cooking time: 12 hours
Servings: 10

Ingredients:
- 2 pounds green peanuts
- 10 cups water
- A pinch of sea salt
- 2 tablespoons Cajun seasoning

Directions:
1. In your slow cooker, mix peanuts with water, salt and Cajun seasoning, stir, cover and cook on Low for 12 hours.
2. Drain, transfer to bowls and serve as a snack.

Enjoy!

Nutrition: calories 90, fat 2, fiber 3, carbs 5, protein 3

Chicken Wings

Preparation time: 10 minutes
Cooking time: 4 hours
Servings: 4

Ingredients:
- ¼ cup coconut aminos
- ¼ cup balsamic vinegar
- 2 garlic cloves, minced
- 2 tablespoon stevia
- 1 teaspoon sriracha sauce
- 3 tablespoons lime juice
- Zest from 1 lime, grated
- 1 teaspoon ginger powder
- 2 teaspoons sesame seeds
- 2 pounds chicken wings
- 2 tablespoons chives, chopped

Directions:
1. In your slow cooker, mix aminos with vinegar, garlic, stevia, sriracha, lime juice, lime zest and ginger and stir well.
2. Add chicken wings, toss well, cover and cook on High for 4 hours.
3. Arrange chicken wings on a platter, sprinkle chives and sesame seeds on top and serve as a casual appetizer.

Enjoy!

Nutrition: calories 212, fat 3, fiber 6, carbs 12, protein 3

Meatballs Appetizer

Preparation time: 10 minutes
Cooking time: 2 hours and 30 minutes
Servings: 6

Ingredients:
- 1 egg
- 1 pound chicken, ground
- ½ teaspoon garlic powder
- ½ teaspoon onion powder
- 2 green onions, chopped
- A pinch of salt and black pepper
- ¾ cup Paleo buffalo sauce

Directions:
1. In a bowl, mix chicken with egg, onion powder, garlic powder, green onions, salt and pepper and stir well.
2. Shape meatballs, add them to your slow cooker, also add buffalo sauce, cover and cook on Low for 2 hours and 30 minutes.
3. Arrange meatballs on a platter and serve them with the sauce on the side.

Enjoy!

Nutrition: calories 221, fat 4, fiber 6, carbs 8, protein 6

Cauliflower and Jalapeno Dip

Preparation time: 10 minutes
Cooking time: 2 hours and 15 minutes
Servings: 6

Ingredients:
- 4 bacon slices, chopped and cooked
- 2 jalapenos, chopped
- ½ cup coconut cream
- 2 cups cauliflower rice
- ¼ cup cashew cheese, grated
- A pinch of salt and black pepper
- 2 tablespoons chives, chopped

Directions:
1. In your slow cooker, mix bacon with jalapenos, coconut cream, cauliflower, salt and pepper, stir, cover and cook on Low for 2 hours.
2. Add cashew cheese and chives, cover and cook on Low for 15 minutes more.
3. Divide into bowls and serve.

Enjoy!

Nutrition: calories 182, fat 3, fiber 3, carbs 7, protein 6

BBQ Kielbasa

Preparation time: 10 minutes
Cooking time: 4 hours
Servings: 6

Ingredients:

- 2 cup tomato sauce
- ½ cup stevia
- 2 teaspoons mustard
- 1 teaspoon hot sauce
- 1 yellow onion, chopped
- 2 pounds kielbasa, sliced

Directions:

1. In your slow cooker, mix kielbasa slices with tomato sauce, stevia, mustard, hot sauce and onion, stirs, cover and cook on Low for 4 hours.
2. Divide kielbasa slices into bowls and serve as a snack.

Enjoy!

Nutrition: calories 200, fat 3, fiber 4, carbs 7, protein 3

Special Mushrooms Appetizer

Preparation time: 10 minutes
Cooking time: 8 hours
Servings: 8

Ingredients:

- 1 shallot, chopped
- 2 garlic cloves, minced
- 2 tablespoons parsley, chopped
- 1 and ½ pounds button mushrooms
- ½ cup chicken stock
- ½ cup coconut cream
- A pinch of salt and black pepper

Directions:

1. In your slow cooker, mix shallot with garlic, parsley, stock, cream, salt and pepper and whisk well.
2. Add mushrooms, cover and cook on Low for 8 hours.
3. Arrange mushrooms on a platter and serve them as an appetizer.

Enjoy!

Nutrition: calories 130, fat 3, fiber 3, carbs 7, protein 3

Nuts Mix

Preparation time: 10 minutes
Cooking time: 4 hours
Servings: 20

Ingredients:
- 4 tablespoons ghee, melted
- 1 ounce Italian seasoning
- 1 teaspoon cinnamon powder
- A pinch of cayenne pepper
- 2 cups cashews
- 2 cups pecans
- 2 cups almonds
- 2 cups walnuts

Directions:
1. In your slow cooker, mix melted ghee with Italian seasoning, cinnamon powder, cayenne, cashews, pecans, almonds and walnuts, toss well, cover and cook on Low for 4 hours.
2. Divide into bowls and serve as a party snack.

Enjoy!

Nutrition: calories 200, fat 4, fiber 3, carbs 14, protein 4

Veggie Salsa

Preparation time: 10 minutes
Cooking time: 5 hours
Servings: 8

Ingredients:
- 2 eggplants, cubed
- 3 celery stalks, chopped
- 1 pound plum tomatoes, chopped
- 1 zucchini, halved and sliced
- 1 red bell pepper, chopped
- 1 cup sweet onion, chopped
- 3 tablespoons tomato paste
- ½ cup raisins
- 1 tablespoon stevia
- 1 teaspoon red pepper flakes, crushed
- ¼ cup basil, chopped
- ¼ cup parsley, chopped
- A pinch of salt and black pepper
- ¼ cup green olives, pitted and chopped
- ¼ cup capers
- 2 tablespoons red wine vinegar

Directions:
1. In your slow cooker, mix eggplants with celery, tomatoes, zucchini, bell pepper, sweet onion, tomato paste, raisins, stevia, pepper flakes, basil, parsley, salt, pepper, olives, capers and vinegar, stir, cover and cook on Low for 5 hours.
2. Divide into small bowls and serve as an appetizer.

Enjoy!

Nutrition: calories 80, fat 1, fiber 2, carbs 6, protein 1

Spinach Dip

Preparation time: 10 minutes
Cooking time: 4 hours
Servings: 24

Ingredients:
- 1 cup sweet onion, chopped
- 4 bacon slices, chopped and cooked
- 28 ounces canned artichoke hearts, chopped
- 10 ounces spinach
- 1 cup red bell pepper, chopped
- 1 cup Paleo mayonnaise
- 8 ounces coconut cream
- 3 garlic cloves, minced
- ½ teaspoon dried mustard

Directions:
1. In your slow cooker, mix onion with bacon, artichokes, spinach, bell pepper, mayo, coconut cream, garlic and dried mustard, stir, cover and cook on Low for 4 hours.
2. Divide into bowls and serve as a dip.

Enjoy!

Nutrition: calories 200, fat 3, fiber 6, carbs 8, protein 3

Caramelized Onion Appetizer

Preparation time: 10 minutes
Cooking time: 6 hours
Servings: 32

Ingredients:
- 1 apple, peeled, cored and chopped
- 2 cups sweet onions, sliced
- 2 tablespoons ghee
- ½ cup cranberries
- ¼ cup balsamic vinegar
- 1 tablespoon stevia
- ½ teaspoon orange zest, grated
- 7 ounces cashew cheese, shredded

Directions:
1. In your slow cooker, mix apples with cranberries, onions, ghee, vinegar, stevia and orange zest, stir, cover and cook on Low for 6 hours.
2. Divide into bowls, sprinkle cashew cheese on to and serve as an appetizer.

Enjoy!

Nutrition: calories 32, fat 2, fiber 1, carbs 3, protein 4

Lemony Snack

Preparation time: 10 minutes
Cooking time: 2 hours and 30 minutes
Servings: 24

Ingredients:
- Cooking spray
- 1 cup walnuts, chopped
- 1 cup pumpkin seeds
- 2 tablespoons dill, dried
- 2 tablespoons olive oil
- 1 teaspoon rosemary, dried
- 1 tablespoon lemon peel, shredded

Directions:
1. Grease your slow cooker with cooking spray.
2. Add walnuts, pumpkin seeds, oil, dill, rosemary and lemon pee, toss, cover and cook on Low for 2 hours and 30 minutes.
3. Divide nuts and seeds into bowls and serve them as a snack.

Enjoy!

Nutrition: calories 100, fat 2, fiber 2, carbs 3, protein 2

Spicy Sausage Appetizer

Preparation time: 10 minutes
Cooking time: 2 hours
Servings: 12

Ingredients:
- 2 pounds spicy pork sausage, sliced
- 18 ounces Paleo apple jelly
- 9 ounces mustard

Directions:
1. In your slow cooker, mix apple jelly with mustard and whisk really well.
2. Add spicy sausage slices, toss really well, cover and cook on Low for 2 hours.
3. Divide sausage slices between bowls and serve them as an appetizer.

Enjoy!

Nutrition: calories 231, fat 4, fiber 6, carbs 7, protein 5

Beef and Pork Party Meatballs

Preparation time: 10 minutes
Cooking time: 5 hours
Servings: 20

Ingredients:

- 1 pound pork sausage, ground
- 1 pound lean beef, ground
- 2 eggs
- ½ cup yellow onion, chopped
- 2 tablespoons parsley, chopped
- A pinch of salt and black pepper
- ½ teaspoon garlic powder
- 12 ounces canned apricot preserves
- ¾ cup BBQ sauce

Directions:

1. In a bowl, mix pork sausage meat with beef meat, eggs, onion, parsley, salt, pepper and garlic powder, stir well and shape 40 meatballs out of this mix.
2. In your slow cooker mix, apricot preserves with BBQ sauce and whisk well.
3. Add meatballs, toss them in the pot, cover and cook on Low for 5 hours.
4. Arrange meatballs, sauce on a platter, and serve them as an appetizer.

Enjoy!

Nutrition: calories 216, fat 4, fiber 6, carbs 8, protein 4

Cocktail Meatballs

Preparation time: 10 minutes
Cooking time: 5 hours
Servings: 30

Ingredients:

- 2 pounds ground beef, ground
- 1 tablespoon coconut flour
- 2 eggs
- ½ cup parsley, chopped
- 1/3 cup tomato paste
- 3 tablespoons onion, chopped
- 2 tablespoon coconut aminos
- A pinch of salt and black pepper
- ¼ teaspoon garlic powder
- 12 ounces chili sauce
- 14 ounces canned cranberry sauce
- 1 tablespoon stevia
- 1 tablespoon lemon juice

Directions:

1. In a bowl, mix beef with coconut flour, eggs, parsley, tomato paste, onion, coconut aminos, salt, pepper and garlic powder, stir well and shape 60 small meatballs out of this mix.
2. In your slow cooker, mix chili sauce with cranberry sauce, stevia and lemon juice and whisk really well.
3. Add meatballs, cover and cook on Low for 5 hours.
4. Arrange meatballs on a platter, drizzle sauce all over and serve as an appetizer.

Enjoy!

Nutrition: calories 251, fat 4, fiber 6, carbs 10, protein 3

Mini Hot Dogs

Preparation time: 10 minutes
Cooking time: 4 hours
Servings: 24

Ingredients:
- 1 pound mini smoked pork sausages
- 12 ounces chili sauce
- 1 cup grape jelly

Directions:
1. In your slow cooker, mix pork sausages with chili sauce and grape jelly, toss, cover and cook on Low for 4 hours.
2. Arrange mini hot dogs on a platter and serve them as an appetizer.

Enjoy!

Nutrition: calories 251, fat 4, fiber 6, carbs 7, protein 3

Chicken Dip

Preparation time: 10 minutes
Cooking time: 3 hours and 30 minutes
Servings: 10

Ingredients:
- 1 pound chicken breast, skinless, boneless and sliced
- 3 tablespoons sriracha sauce
- ¼ cup chicken stock
- 2 tablespoons stevia
- 1 teaspoon hot sauce
- 8 ounces coconut cream

Directions:
1. In your slow cooker, mix chicken with sriracha sauce, stock, stevia and hot sauce, stir, cover and cook on High for 3 hours.
2. Shred meat, return to pot, also add coconut cream, cover and cook on High for 30 minutes more.
3. Divide into bowls and serve as a party dip.

Enjoy!

Nutrition: calories 231, fat 3, fiber 6, carbs 10, protein 3

Crab Dip

Preparation time: 10 minutes
Cooking time: 2 hours
Servings: 6

Ingredients:

- 4 ounces coconut cream
- 1 pound crab meat
- 1 jalapeno, chopped
- 1 red bell pepper, chopped
- 4 tablespoons lemon juice
- 2 garlic cloves, minced
- ½ teaspoon mustard powder

Directions:

1. In your slow cooker, mix coconut cream with crab meat, jalapeno, bell pepper, lemon juice, garlic and mustard, stir, cover and cook on High for 2 hours.
2. Stir again, divide into bowls and serve as a party dip.

Enjoy!

Nutrition: calories 182, fat 3, fiber 6, carbs 7, protein 3

Tomato Dip

Preparation time: 10 minutes
Cooking time: 5 hours
Servings: 12

Ingredients:

- 8 pounds tomatoes, peeled and chopped
- 2 sweet onions, chopped
- 6 garlic cloves, minced
- 6 ounces tomato paste
- ¼ cup white vinegar
- 2 tablespoons coconut sugar
- 1 and ½ tablespoons Italian seasoning
- A pinch of salt and black pepper
- ½ cup basil, chopped
- 1 tablespoon thyme, chopped

Directions:

1. In your slow cooker, mix tomatoes with onions, garlic, tomato paste, vinegar, coconut sugar, Italian seasoning, salt, pepper, basil and thyme, stir, cover and cook on High for 5 hours.
2. Blend using an immersion blender, divide into bowls and serve as a party dip.

Enjoy!

Nutrition: calories 182, fat 3, fiber 6, carbs 8, protein 3

Paleo Slow Cooker Fish and Seafood Recipes

Flavored Tilapia

Preparation time: 10 minutes
Cooking time: 2 hours
Servings: 4

Ingredients:
- 1 asparagus bunch, spears trimmed
- 12 tablespoons lemon juice
- 4 tilapia fillets
- A pinch of lemon pepper
- 2 tablespoons olive oil

Directions:
1. Divide tilapia fillets on 4 parchment paper pieces.
2. Divide asparagus on top, drizzle the lemon juice and sprinkle a pinch of pepper.
3. Drizzle the oil all over, wrap fish and asparagus and place in your slow cooker.
4. Cover and cook on High for 2 hours.
5. Unwrap fish, divide between plates and serve.

Enjoy!

Nutrition: calories 200, fat 3, fiber 1, carbs 8, protein 6

Special Seafood Chowder

Preparation time: 10 minutes
Cooking time: 8 hours and 30 minutes
Servings: 4

Ingredients:
- 2 cups water
- ½ fennel bulb, chopped
- 2 sweet potatoes, cubed
- 1 yellow onion, chopped
- 2 bay leaves
- 1 tablespoon thyme, dried
- 1 celery rib, chopped
- Black pepper to the taste
- A pinch of cayenne pepper
- 1 bottle clam juice
- 2 tablespoons tapioca powder
- 1 cup coconut milk
- 1 pounds salmon fillets, cubed
- 5 sea scallops, halved
- 24 shrimp, peeled and deveined
- ¼ cup parsley, chopped

Directions:
1. In your slow cooker, mix water with fennel, potatoes, onion, bay leaves, thyme, celery, clam juice, cayenne, black pepper and tapioca powdered, stir, cover and cook on Low for 8 hours.
2. Add salmon, coconut milk, scallops, shrimp and parsley, cover and cook on Low for 30 minutes more.
3. Ladle chowder into bowls and serve.

Enjoy!

Nutrition: calories 354, fat 10, fiber 2, carbs 10, protein 12

Elegant Salmon Dish

Preparation time: 10 minutes
Cooking time: 3 hours
Servings: 2

Ingredients:
- 2 medium salmon fillets
- A pinch of sea salt
- Black pepper to the taste
- 2 tablespoons coconut aminos
- 2 tablespoons maple syrup
- 16 ounces mixed broccoli and cauliflower florets
- 2 tablespoons lemon juice
- 1 teaspoon sesame seeds

Directions:
1. Put the cauliflower and broccoli florets in your slow cooker and top with salmon fillets.
2. In a bowl, mix maple syrup with aminos and lemon juice and whisk really well.
3. Pour this over salmon fillets, season with black pepper to the taste, sprinkle sesame seeds on top and cook on Low for 3 hours.
4. Divide everything between plates and serve.

Enjoy!

Nutrition: calories 230, fat 4, fiber 2, carbs 7, protein 6

Seafood Stew

Preparation time: 10 minutes
Cooking time: 3 hours and 30 minutes
Servings: 6

Ingredients:
- 3 garlic cloves, minced
- 28 ounces canned tomatoes, crushed
- 1 pound sweet potatoes, peeled and cubed
- 4 cups veggie stock
- 1 small yellow onion, chopped
- 1 teaspoon cilantro, dried
- 1 teaspoon thyme, dried
- 1 teaspoon basil, dried
- A pinch of sea salt
- Black pepper to the taste
- ¼ teaspoon red pepper flakes
- A pinch of cayenne pepper
- 2 pounds mixed scallops and peeled and deveined shrimp

Directions:
1. Put tomatoes in your slow cooker.
2. Add garlic, sweet potatoes, stock, onion, cilantro, thyme, basil, salt, pepper, cayenne and pepper flakes, stir, cover and cook on High for 3 hours.
3. Add scallops and shrimp, stir gently, cover and cook on High for 30 minutes more.
4. Divide into bowls and serve.

Enjoy!

Nutrition: calories 230, fat 3, fiber 2, carbs 8, protein 6

Divine Shrimp Scampi

Preparation time: 10 minutes
Cooking time: 1 hour and 30 minutes
Servings: 4

Ingredients:
- 2 tablespoons olive oil
- ¼ cup chicken stock
- 1 tablespoon garlic, minced
- 2 tablespoons parsley, chopped
- Juice of ½ lemon
- A pinch of sea salt
- Black pepper to the taste
- 1 pound shrimp, peeled and deveined

Directions:
1. Put the oil in your slow cooker.
2. Add stock, garlic, parsley, lemon juice, salt and pepper and whisk really well.
3. Add shrimp, stir, cover and cook on High for 1 hour and 30 minutes.
4. Divide into bowls and serve.

Enjoy!

Nutrition: calories 140, fat 4, fiber 3, carbs 9, protein 3

Steamed Pompano

Preparation time: 10 minutes
Cooking time: 1 hour
Servings: 4

Ingredients:
- 2 tablespoons agave nectar
- 1 pompano
- 2 tablespoons coconut aminos
- ¼ cup sesame oil
- ¼ cup veggie stock
- 1 small ginger piece, grated
- 6 garlic cloves, minced
- 2 tablespoons Paleo Worcestershire sauce
- 1 bunch leeks, chopped
- 1 bunch cilantro, chopped

Directions:
1. Put the oil in your slow cooker.
2. Add leeks and top with the fish.
3. In a bowl, mix stock with ginger, garlic, cilantro and coconut aminos and whisk well.
4. Add this to the pot as well, cover and cook on High for 1 hour.
5. Divide fish among plates and serve with the sauce drizzled on top.

Enjoy!

Nutrition: calories 300, fat 8, fiber 2, carbs 8, protein 6

Special Poached Milkfish

Preparation time: 10 minutes
Cooking time: 4 hours
Servings: 2

Ingredients:
- 1 pound milkfish
- 6 garlic cloves, minced
- 1 small ginger pieces, chopped
- ½ tablespoon black peppercorns
- 1 cup pineapple juice
- 1 cup pineapple, chopped
- ¼ cup white vinegar
- 4 jalapeno peppers, chopped
- A pinch of sea salt
- Black pepper to the taste

Directions:
1. Put the fish in your slow cooker and season with a pinch of salt and some black pepper.
2. Add garlic, ginger, peppercorns, pineapple juice, pineapple chunks, vinegar and jalapenos.
3. Stir gently, cover and cook on Low for 4 hours.
4. Divide fish between 2 plates and top with the pineapple mix.

Enjoy!

Nutrition: calories 240, fat 4, fiber 4, carbs 8, protein 3

Great Catfish Dish

Preparation time: 10 minutes
Cooking time: 6 hours
Servings: 3

Ingredients:
- 1 catfish, cut into 3 pieces
- 3 red chili peppers, chopped
- ½ cup coconut sugar
- ¼ cup coconut water
- 1 tablespoon coconut aminos
- 1 shallot, minced
- A small ginger piece, grated
- A handful coriander, chopped

Directions:
1. Put the catfish in your slow cooker.
2. Heat up a pan with the coconut sugar over medium high heat and stir until it caramelizes.
3. Add aminos, shallot, ginger, coconut water and chili pepper, stir and pour over the fish.
4. Add coriander, stir again, cover and cook on Low for 6 hours.
5. Divide between plates and serve with the sauce from the slow cooker drizzled on top.

Enjoy!

Nutrition: calories 200, fat 4, fiber 4, carbs 8, protein 10

Stylish Tuna Dish

Preparation time: 10 minutes
Cooking time: 4 hours and 10 minutes
Servings: 2

Ingredients:
- ½ pound tuna loin, cubed
- 1 garlic clove, minced
- 4 jalapeno peppers, chopped
- 1 cup olive oil
- 3 red chili peppers, chopped
- 2 teaspoons black peppercorns, ground
- A pinch of sea salt
- Black pepper to the taste

Directions:
1. Put the oil in your slow cooker, add chili peppers, jalapenos, peppercorns, salt, pepper and garlic and whisk.
2. Cover and cook on Low for 4 hours.
3. Add tuna cubes, stir again and cook on High for 10 minutes more.
4. Divide between plates and serve.

Enjoy!

Nutrition: calories 200, fat 4, fiber 3, carbs 10, protein 4

Tasty Braised Squid

Preparation time: 10 minutes
Cooking time: 7 hours
Servings: 4

Ingredients:
- 1 pound squid, cleaned and cut into rings
- 1/2 cup coconut sugar
- 1 small ginger piece, grated
- 1 garlic head, crushed
- 3 tablespoons coconut aminos
- 1/4 cup veggie stock
- 2 leeks stalks, chopped
- 2 bay leaves
- Black pepper to the taste

Directions:
1. Put the squid in your slow cooker.
2. Add sugar, ginger, garlic, aminos, leeks, stock, black pepper and bay leaves, stir, cover and cook on Low for 8 hours.
3. Divide into bowls and serve right away.

Enjoy!

Nutrition: calories 190, fat 2, fiber 4, carbs 7, protein 5

Seabass and Coconut Cream

Preparation time: 10 minutes
Cooking time: 1 hour and 30 minutes
Servings: 2

Ingredients:

- 1 pound sea bass
- 2 scallion stalks, chopped
- 1 small ginger piece, grated
- 1 tablespoon coconut aminos
- 2 cups coconut cream
- 4 bok choy stalks, chopped
- 3 jalapeno peppers, chopped
- A pinch of sea salt
- Black pepper to the taste

Directions:

1. Put coconut cream in your slow cooker.
2. Add ginger, aminos, scallions, a pinch of salt, black pepper and jalapenos.
3. Stir, top with the fish and bok choy, cover and cook on High for 1 hour and 30 minutes.
4. Divide fish and cream between 2 plates and serve.

Enjoy!

Nutrition: calories 200, fat 3, fiber 3, carbs 8, protein 5

Wonderful Shrimp and Crawfish

Preparation time: 10 minutes
Cooking time: 5 hours and 6 minutes
Servings: 8

Ingredients:

- 1 pound shrimp, peeled and deveined
- ½ cup yellow onions, chopped
- 2 celery stalks, chopped
- ½ cup red bell pepper, chopped
- 4 green onions, chopped
- ¼ cup olive oil
- 1 tablespoon tapioca flour
- 1 and ½ tablespoons garlic, minced
- 10 ounces canned tomatoes and chilies, chopped
- 1 pound crawfish tails, cooked and peeled
- 2/3 cup water
- 6 ounces canned sugar free tomato paste
- ½ teaspoon oregano, dried
- ½ teaspoon basil, dried
- ½ teaspoon thyme, dried
- Black pepper to the taste
- A pinch of red pepper, crushed
- ½ cup parsley, chopped

Directions:

1. Heat up a pan with the oil over medium high heat, add onions, bell pepper, celery and green onions, stir and cook for a couple of minutes.
2. Add garlic and tomatoes, stir and transfer everything to your slow cooker.
3. Add tomato paste, water, flour, black pepper, oregano, basil, red pepper and thyme, stir, cover and cook on Low for 4 hours.
4. Add shrimp, crawfish and parsley, stir, cover and cook on Low for 1 more hour.
5. Divide into bowls and serve.

Enjoy!

Nutrition: calories 240, fat 2, fiber 2, carbs 7, protein 2

Salmon with Cilantro And Lime

Preparation time: 10 minutes
Cooking time: 2 hours and 30 minutes
Servings: 4

Ingredients:
- 2 garlic cloves, minced
- 4 salmon fillets
- ¾ cup cilantro, chopped
- 3 tablespoons lime juice
- 1 tablespoon olive oil
- A pinch of sea salt
- Black pepper to the taste

Directions:
1. Grease your slow cooker with the oil and place salmon fillets inside, skin side down.
2. Add garlic, cilantro, lime juice, salt and pepper, cover and cook on Low for 2 hours and 30 minutes.
3. Divide salmon fillets on plates, drizzle the juices from the slow cooker all over and serve.

Enjoy!

Nutrition: calories 180, fat 3, fiber 2, carbs 4, protein 8

Jamaican Salmon

Preparation time: 10 minutes
Cooking time: 2 hours
Servings: 2

Ingredients:
- 1 medium salmon fillets
- A pinch of nutmeg, ground
- A pinch of cloves, ground
- A pinch of ginger powder
- A pinch of sea salt
- 2 teaspoons coconut sugar
- 1 teaspoon onion powder
- ¼ teaspoon chipotle chili powder
- ½ teaspoon cayenne pepper
- Black pepper to the taste
- ½ teaspoon cinnamon, ground
- 1/8 teaspoon thyme, dried

Directions:
1. In a bowl, mix salmon fillets with nutmeg, cloves, ginger, salt, coconut sugar, onion powder, chili powder, cayenne black pepper, cinnamon and thyme.
2. Rub fish with this mix, arrange fish on 2 tin foil pieces, wrap, place in your slow cooker, cover and cook on Low for 2 hours.
3. Unwrap fish, divide between plates and serve with a side salad.

Enjoy!

Nutrition: calories 220, fat 4, fiber 2, carbs 7, protein 4

Simple Clams

Preparation time: 10 minutes
Cooking time: 6 hours
Servings: 4

Ingredients:

- 21 ounces canned clams, chopped
- 1/3 cup coconut milk
- 4 eggs, whisked
- 2 tablespoons olive oil
- 1/3 cup green bell pepper, chopped
- ½ cup yellow onion, chopped
- Black pepper to the taste
- A pinch of sea salt

Directions:

1. Put clams in your slow cooker.
2. Add milk, eggs, oil, onion, bell pepper, a pinch of salt and black pepper.
3. Stir, cover and cook on Low for 6 hours.
4. Divide into bowls and serve.

Enjoy!

Nutrition: calories 190, fat 4, fiber 2, carbs 6, protein 7

Delicious Clam Chowder

Preparation time: 10 minutes
Cooking time: 3 hours and 30 minutes
Servings: 6

Ingredients:

- 6 bacon slices, cooked and chopped
- 1 yellow onion, chopped
- 3 carrots, chopped
- 13 ounces canned clams, chopped
- 2 sweet potatoes, chopped
- 1 and ¾ cups water
- 1 teaspoon Paleo Worcestershire sauce
- ¼ cup tapioca flour
- 24 ounces canned coconut milk

Directions:

1. In your slow cooker, mix water with clams, carrots, onion, bacon, potatoes and Worcestershire sauce, stir, cover and cook on High for 3 hours.
2. Add coconut milk mixed with tapioca flour, stir and cook on High for 30 minutes more.
3. Divide chowder into bowls and serve.

Enjoy!

Nutrition: calories 140, fat 10, fiber 1, carbs 8, protein 10

Easy Seafood Soup

Preparation time: 10 minutes
Cooking time: 3 hours
Servings: 12

Ingredients:

- 10 ounces canned coconut cream
- 2 cups veggie stock
- 2 cups tomato sauce
- 1 cup Paleo shrimp cocktail sauce
- 12 ounces canned crab meat
- 1 and ½ cups water
- 1 pound small shrimp, peeled and deveined
- 1 pound jumbo shrimp, peeled and deveined
- 1 yellow onion, chopped
- 1 cup carrots, chopped
- 4 tilapia fillets, cubed
- 2 celery stalks, chopped
- 3 kale stalks, chopped
- 1 bay leaf
- 2 garlic cloves, minced
- A pinch of sea salt
- ½ teaspoon cloves, ground
- 1 teaspoon rosemary, dried
- 1 teaspoon thyme, dried

Directions:

1. In your slow cooker, mix coconut cream with stock, tomato sauce, shrimp cocktail sauce and water and stir.
2. Add small and jumbo shrimp, fish cubes, onion, carrots, celery, kale, garlic, bay leaf, salt, cloves, thyme and rosemary, stir, cover and cook on Low for 3 hours.
3. Stir soup again, ladle into bowls and serve.

Enjoy!

Nutrition: calories 220, fat 3, fiber 3, carbs 8, protein 13

Easy Seafood Gumbo

Preparation time: 10 minutes
Cooking time: 6 hours
Servings: 4

Ingredients:

- 1 pound shrimp, peeled and deveined
- 2 pounds mussels, cleaned and debearded
- 28 ounces canned clams
- 1 yellow onion, chopped
- 10 ounces canned tomato paste

Directions:

1. In your slow cooker, mix shrimp with mussels, clams, onion and tomato paste, stir, cover and cook on Low for 6 hours.
2. Ladle into bowls and serve.

Enjoy!

Nutrition: calories 150, fat 3, fiber 2, carbs 7, protein 5

Coconut Curry Shrimp

Preparation time: 10 minutes
Cooking time: 4 hours and 30 minutes
Servings: 2

Ingredients:

- 1 small yellow onion, chopped
- 15 baby carrots
- 2 garlic cloves, minced
- 1 small green bell pepper, chopped
- 8 ounces canned coconut milk
- 3 tablespoons tomato paste
- ½ teaspoon red pepper, crushed
- ¾ tablespoons curry powder
- ¾ tablespoon tapioca flour
- 1 pound shrimp, cooked, peeled and deveined

Directions:

1. In your food processor, mix onion with garlic, bell pepper, tomato paste, coconut milk, red pepper and curry powder, blend well and add to your slow cooker.
2. Add baby carrots, stir, cover and cook on Low for 4 hours.
3. Add tapioca, stir, cover and cook on Low for 15 minutes more.
4. Add shrimp, stir and cook on Low for 15 minutes more.
5. Divide into bowls and serve.

Enjoy!

Nutrition: calories 200, fat 4, fiber 3, carbs 4, protein 5

Lemon and Dill Trout

Preparation time: 10 minutes
Cooking time: 2 hours
Servings: 4

Ingredients:

- 2 lemons, sliced
- ¼ cup low sodium chicken stock
- A pinch of sea salt
- Black pepper to the taste
- 2 tablespoons dill, chopped
- 12 ounces spinach
- 4 medium trout

Directions:

1. Put the stock in your slow cooker and add the fish inside as well.
2. Season with a pinch of salt and black pepper to the taste, top with lemon slices, dill and spinach, cover and cook on High for 2 hours.
3. Divide fish, lemon and spinach between plates and drizzle some of the juice from the pot all over.

Enjoy!

Nutrition: calories 240, fat 5, fiber 4, carbs 9, protein 14

Elegant Tilapia and Asparagus

Preparation time: 10 minutes
Cooking time: 2 hours
Servings: 4

Ingredients:
- 4 tilapia fillets, boneless
- 1 bundle asparagus
- 12 tablespoons lemon juice
- A pinch of lemon pepper seasoning
- 2 tablespoons olive oil

Directions:
1. Divide tilapia fillets on tin foil pieces.
2. Top each tilapia with asparagus spears, lemon juice, lemon pepper and oil and wrap them.
3. Arrange tilapia fillets in your slow cooker, cover and cook on High for 2 hours.
4. Unwrap tilapia and divide fish and asparagus between plates.

Enjoy!

Nutrition: calories 172, fat 3, fiber 6, carbs 7, protein 3

Seafood Chowder

Preparation time: 10 minutes
Cooking time: 8 hours
Servings: 4

Ingredients:
- ½ fennel bulb, cored and chopped
- 2 bay leaves
- 1 yellow onion, chopped
- 1 celery rib, chopped
- 1 tablespoon thyme, chopped
- A pinch of salt and black pepper
- 3 ounces clam juice
- 1 cup coconut cream
- 1 pound salmon fillet, skinless, boneless and cut into medium chunks
- 5 sea scallops, halved
- 24 shrimp, peeled and deveined
- ¼ cup parsley, chopped

Directions:
1. In your slow cooker, mix fennel with bay leaves, onion, celery, thyme, salt, pepper, clam juice, salmon, shrimp and coconut cream, stir, cover and cook on Low for 8 hours.
2. Add parsley, stir, divide into bowls and serve.

Enjoy!

Nutrition: calories 172, fat 3, fiber 7, carbs 13, protein 3

Asian Style Salmon

Preparation time: 10 minutes
Cooking time: 3 hours
Servings: 4

Ingredients:
- 4 salmon fillets, boneless
- 1 red bell pepper, cut into medium strips
- 1 tomato, cut into medium wedges
- 1 carrot, cut into matchsticks
- 2 tablespoons coconut aminos
- 2 tablespoons stevia
- 2 tablespoons lemon juice
- 1 teaspoon sesame seeds

Directions:
1. In your slow cooker, mix salmon with red bell pepper, tomato carrot, aminos, stevia and lemon juice, toss, cover and cook on Low for 3 hours.
2. Add sesame seeds, divide Asian fish mix between plates and serve.

Enjoy!

Nutrition: calories 162, fat 4, fiber 7, carbs 8, protein 3

Tasty Seafood Stew

Preparation time: 10 minutes
Cooking time: 7 hours
Servings: 4

Ingredients:
- 28 ounces canned tomatoes, crushed
- 4 cups veggie stock
- 3 garlic cloves, minced
- 1 pound sweet potatoes, cubed
- ½ cup yellow onion, chopped
- 1 teaspoon thyme, dried
- 1 teaspoon cilantro, dried
- 1 teaspoon basil, dried
- A pinch of salt and black pepper
- A pinch of red pepper flakes, crushed
- 2 pounds favorite seafood

Directions:
1. In your slow cooker, mix tomatoes with stock, garlic, sweet potatoes, onion, thyme, cilantro, basil, salt, pepper and pepper flakes, stir, cover and cook on Low for 6 hours.
2. Add seafood, stir, cover and cook on High for 1 more hour.
3. Divide stew into bowls and serve.

Enjoy!

Nutrition: calories 200, fat 4, fiber 4, carbs 6, protein 3

Shrimp Mix

Preparation time: 10 minutes
Cooking time: 2 hours and 30 minutes
Servings: 4

Ingredients:
- 1 cup chicken stock
- 2 tablespoons olive oil
- 2 teaspoons parsley, chopped
- 2 teaspoons garlic, minced
- 20 shrimp, peeled and deveined

Directions:
1. In your slow cooker, mix stock with oil, parsley, garlic and shrimp, toss, cover and cook on Low for 2 hours and 30 minutes.
2. Divide into bowls and serve.

Enjoy!

Nutrition: calories 162, fat 2, fiber 6, carbs 9, protein 2

Fish and Tomatoes

Preparation time: 10 minutes
Cooking time: 1 hour and 30 minutes
Servings: 4

Ingredients:
- 1 pound cod fillets, skinless and boneless
- 1 yellow onion, chopped
- 1 red bell pepper, chopped
- 3 garlic cloves, minced
- 15 ounces canned tomatoes, chopped
- 1 tablespoons rosemary, chopped
- ¼ cup veggie stock
- A pinch of red pepper flakes, crushed
- A pinch of salt and black pepper

Directions:
1. In your slow cooker, mix tomatoes with onion, bell pepper, garlic, rosemary, stock, pepper flakes, salt and pepper and stir.
2. Add fish fillets on top, cover and cook on Low for 1 hour and 30 minutes.
3. Divide everything between plates and serve.

Enjoy!

Nutrition: calories 200, fat 4, fiber 3, carbs 7, protein 4

Italian Seafood Stew

Preparation time: 10 minutes
Cooking time: 4 hours and 30 minutes
Servings: 8

Ingredients:

- 29 ounces canned tomatoes, chopped
- 2 yellow onions, chopped
- 2 celery ribs, chopped
- 6 ounces tomato paste
- ½ cup veggie stock
- 4 garlic cloves, minced
- 1 tablespoon red vinegar
- 2 teaspoons Italian seasoning
- 2 tablespoons olive oil
- 1 pound haddock fillets, skinless, boneless and cubed
- 1 pound shrimp, peeled and deveined
- 6 ounces canned clams
- 6 ounces crab meat
- 2 tablespoons parsley, chopped

Directions:

1. In your slow cooker, mix tomatoes with onions, celery, tomato paste, stock, garlic, Italian seasoning and oil, whisk well, cover and cook on Low for 4 hours.
2. Add haddock, clams, shrimp, crab and parsley, stir gently, cover and cook on Low for 30 minutes more.
3. Divide into bowls and serve.

Enjoy!

Nutrition: calories 205, fat 4, fiber 3, carbs 14, protein 26

Salmon with Onions and Carrots

Preparation time: 10 minutes
Cooking time: 9 hours
Servings: 4

Ingredients:

- 16 ounces baby carrots
- 4 onions, chopped
- 3 tablespoons olive oil
- 4 garlic cloves, minced
- 4 salmon fillets, boneless
- ½ teaspoon dill, chopped
- A pinch of salt and black pepper

Directions:

1. In your slow cooker, mix oil with carrots, onions and garlic, stir, cover and cook on Low for 7 hours.
2. Add salmon, salt, pepper and dill, cover and cook on Low for 2 hours more.
3. Divide everything between plates and serve.

Enjoy!

Nutrition: calories 200, fat 3, fiber 6, carbs 8, protein 2

Slow Cooker Shrimp Dish

Preparation time: 10 minutes
Cooking time: 8 hours
Servings: 8

Ingredients:
- 4 cups veggie stock
- 2 tablespoons Italian seasoning
- 1 pound sausage, sliced
- A pinch of salt and black pepper
- 2 pound shrimp, deveined
- 2 tablespoons parsley, chopped
- 4 tablespoons olive oil

Directions:
1. In your slow cooker, mix stock with Italian seasoning, sausage, salt, pepper, oil and shrimp, toss, cover and cook on Low for 8 hours.
2. Add parsley, stir, divide into bowls and serve.

Enjoy!

Nutrition: calories 172, fat 3, fiber 5, carbs 7, protein 3

Shrimp Soup

Preparation time: 10 minutes
Cooking time: 3 hours
Servings: 6

Ingredients:
- 1 and ½ cups celery, chopped
- 1 cup green bell pepper, chopped
- 1 and ½ cups onions, chopped
- 8 ounces tomato sauce
- 28 ounces canned tomatoes, chopped
- 28 ounces chicken stock
- 2 garlic cloves, minced
- A pinch of salt and black pepper
- ¼ cup red vinegar
- 1 pound shrimp, deveined

Directions:
1. In your slow cooker, mix celery with bell pepper, onion, tomato sauce, tomatoes, stock, garlic, salt, pepper, vinegar and shrimp, stir, cover and cook on High for 3 hours.
2. Ladle soup into bowls and serve.

Enjoy!

Nutrition: calories 162, fat 3, fiber 3, carbs 9, protein 3

Cod with Tomatoes and Olives

Preparation time: 10 minutes
Cooking time: 2 hours
Servings: 4

Ingredients:
- 4 cod fillets, boneless
- 1 cup black olives, pitted and chopped
- 1 tablespoon olive oil
- 1 garlic clove, minced
- ½ cup veggie stock
- A pinch of salt and black pepper
- 1 pound cherry tomatoes, halved
- A pinch of thyme, dried

Directions:
1. In your slow cooker, mix cod with black olives, oil, garlic, stock, salt, pepper, cherry tomatoes and thyme, cover and cook on High for 2 hours.
2. Divide everything between plates and serve.

Enjoy!

Nutrition: calories 200, fat 3, fiber 4, carbs 8, protein 17

Cod Curry

Preparation time: 10 minutes
Cooking time: 2 hours
Servings: 6

Ingredients:
- 6 cod fillets, skinless, boneless and cut into medium cubes
- 1 tomato, chopped
- 14 ounces coconut milk
- 2 yellow onions, sliced
- 2 green bell peppers, chopped
- 2 garlic cloves, minced
- ½ teaspoon turmeric powder
- 6 curry leaves
- A pinch of salt and black pepper
- 2 teaspoons cumin, ground
- 2 tablespoons lemon juice
- 1 tablespoons coriander, ground
- 1 tablespoon ginger, grated
- 1 teaspoon hot pepper flakes

Directions:
1. In your slow cooker, mix fish cubes with tomato, coconut milk, onions, green bell peppers, garlic, curry leaves, turmeric, salt, pepper, cumin, lemon juice, coriander, ginger and pepper flakes, toss a bit, cover and cook on High for 2 hours.
2. Divide into bowls and serve.

Enjoy!

Nutrition: calories 201, fat 7, fiber 3, carbs 12, protein 13

Salmon Dinner Mix

Preparation time: 10 minutes
Cooking time: 2 hours
Servings: 4

Ingredients:

- 3 salmon fillets, skin on and boneless
- Zest from 1 lemon, grated
- 4 scallions, chopped
- 3 black peppercorns
- ½ teaspoon fennel seeds
- Salt and black pepper to the taste
- 1 bay leaf
- 1 teaspoon white wine vinegar
- 2 cups chicken stock
- ¼ cup dill, chopped

Directions:

1. In your slow cooker, mix lemon zest with scallions, peppercorns, fennel, salt, pepper, bay leaf, vinegar, stock and dill and stir.
2. Add salmon fillets, cover and cook on High for 2 hours.
3. Divide salmon and scallions mix from the pot on plates and serve.

Enjoy!

Nutrition: calories 152, fat 3, fiber 2, carbs 4, protein 12

Salmon, Carrots and Broccoli

Preparation time: 10 minutes
Cooking time: 2 hours
Servings: 2

Ingredients:

- 2 salmon fillets, skin on
- 1 bay leaf
- 1 cup veggie stock
- 1 cinnamon stick
- 3 cloves
- 1 tablespoon olive oil
- 1 cup baby carrots
- 2 cups broccoli florets
- Salt and black pepper to the taste

Directions:

1. In your slow cooker, mix stock with bay leaf, cinnamon, cloves, oil, carrots, broccoli, salt and pepper and toss.
2. Add salmon, toss a bit, cover and cook on High for 2 hours.
3. Divide salmon and veggies on plates, drizzle some of the cooking juices on top and serve.

Enjoy!

Nutrition: calories 200, fat 4, fiber 6, carbs 14, protein 16

Salmon Fillets and Lemon Sauce

Preparation time: 10 minutes
Cooking time: 2 hours
Servings: 4

Ingredients:

- 4 salmon fillets
- 2 tablespoons chili pepper
- Juice of 1 lemon
- 1 lemon, sliced
- 1 cup veggie stock
- 1 teaspoon sweet paprika
- 1 teaspoon basil, dried
- Salt and black pepper to the taste

Directions:

1. In your slow cooker, mix chili pepper with lemon juice, stock, paprika, basil, salt and pepper and whisk.
2. Add salmon fillets, top them with lemon slices, cover and cook on High for 2 hours.
3. Divide salmon on plates, drizzle sauce from the Crockpot all over and serve.

Enjoy!

Nutrition: calories 200, fat 4, fiber 7, carbs 16, protein 3

Salmon and Special Sauce

Preparation time: 10 minutes
Cooking time: 2 hours
Servings: 6

Ingredients:

- 6 salmon steaks
- 2 tablespoons olive oil
- 4 leeks, sliced
- 2 garlic cloves, minced
- 2 tablespoons parsley, chopped
- 1 cup clam juice
- 2 tablespoons lemon juice
- Salt and white pepper to the taste
- 2 cups raspberries
- 1/3 cup dill, chopped

Directions:

1. In your slow cooker, mix oil with leeks, garlic, parsley, clam juice, lemon juice, salt, pepper, raspberries and dill and stir,
2. Add salmon steaks on top, cover and cook on High for 2 hours.
3. Divide salmon and raspberry sauce between plates and serve.

Enjoy!

Nutrition: calories 321, fat 5, fiber 8, carbs 14, protein 16

Spicy Mackerel

Preparation time: 10 minutes
Cooking time: 2 hours and 30 minutes
Servings: 4

Ingredients:
- 18 ounces mackerel, cut into pieces
- 3 garlic cloves, minced
- 8 shallots, chopped
- 1 teaspoon shrimp powder
- 1 teaspoon turmeric powder
- 1 tablespoon chili paste
- 2 lemongrass sticks, halved
- 1 small piece of ginger, chopped
- 3 and ½ ounces water
- 5 tablespoons olive oil
- 1 and 1/3 tablespoons tamarind paste
- Salt to the taste

Directions:
1. In your blender, mix garlic with shallots, chili paste, turmeric powder and shrimp powder, blend well and add to slow cooker.
2. Also add fish, oil, ginger, lemongrass, tamarind, water and salt, stir, cover and cook on Low for 2 hours and 30 minutes.
3. Divide between plates and serve.

Enjoy!

Nutrition: calories 172, fat 8, fiber 4, carbs 12, protein 16

Mussels Stew

Preparation time: 10 minutes
Cooking time: 2 hours
Servings: 4

Ingredients:
- 2 pounds mussels, scrubbed
- 2 tablespoons olive oil
- 1 yellow onion, chopped
- 1 teaspoon parsley, dried
- ½ teaspoon red pepper flakes, crushed
- 2 teaspoons garlic, minced
- 14 ounces tomatoes, chopped
- ½ cup chicken stock

Directions:
1. In your slow cooker, mix mussels with oil, onion parsley, pepper flakes, garlic, tomatoes and stock, stir, cover and cook on High for 2 hours.
2. Divide into bowls and serve.

Enjoy!

Nutrition: calories 100, fat 2, fiber 3, carbs 7, protein 2

Squid Stew

Preparation time: 10 minutes
Cooking time: 2 hours
Servings: 4

Ingredients:

- 17 ounces squid
- 1 and ½ tablespoons red chili powder
- Salt and black pepper to the taste
- ¼ teaspoon turmeric powder
- 2 cups veggie stock
- 4 garlic cloves, minced
- 1 teaspoon ginger powder
- ½ teaspoons cumin, ground
- 3 tablespoons olive oil
- ¼ teaspoon mustard seeds, toasted

Directions:

1. Put squids in your slow cooker, add chili powder, salt, pepper, turmeric, stock, garlic, ginger, cumin, oil and mustard seeds, stir, cover and cook on High for 2 hours.

Enjoy!

Nutrition: calories 241, fat 1, fiber 7, carbs 12, protein 3

Lemony Mackerel

Preparation time: 10 minutes
Cooking time: 2 hours
Servings: 4

Ingredients:

- 4 mackerels
- Juice from 1 lemon
- Zest from 1 lemon, grated
- 1 tablespoon chives, finely chopped
- Salt and black pepper to the taste
- 2 tablespoons ghee
- 1 tablespoon olive oil
- 1 cup veggie stock
- Lemon wedges for serving

Directions:

1. In your instant pot, mix ghee with oil.
2. Add mackerels, salt and pepper and rub well.
3. Also, add stock, chives, lemon juice and lemon zest, cover and cook on Low for 2 hours.
4. Divide mackerel between plates and serve with lemon wedges on the side.

Enjoy!

Nutrition: calories 162, fat 4, fiber 7, carbs 8, protein 4

Paleo Slow Cooker Poultry Recipes

Delicious Pulled Chicken

Preparation time: 10 minutes
Cooking time: 6 hours
Servings: 2

Ingredients:

- 2 tomatoes, chopped
- 2 red onions, chopped
- 2 chicken breasts
- 2 garlic cloves, minced
- 1 tablespoon maple syrup
- 1 teaspoon chili powder
- 1 teaspoon basil, dried
- 3 tablespoons water
- 1 teaspoon cloves
- Lettuce leaves for serving

Directions:

1. In your slow cooker mix onion with tomatoes, chicken, garlic, maple syrup, chili powder, basil, water and cloves, toss well, cover and cook on Low for 6 hours.
2. Shred chicken and divide it along with the veggies on lettuce leaves.
3. Serve right away!

Enjoy!

Nutrition: calories 200, fat 3, fiber 3, carbs 7, protein 6

Chicken Chili

Preparation time: 10 minutes
Cooking time: 7 hours
Servings: 4

Ingredients:

- 16 ounces jarred Paleo salsa
- 8 chicken thighs
- 1 yellow onion, chopped
- 16 ounces canned tomatoes, chopped
- 1 red bell pepper, chopped
- 2 tablespoons chili powder

Directions:

1. Put the salsa in your slow cooker.
2. Add chicken, onion, tomatoes, bell pepper and chili powder, stir, cover and cook on Low for 7 hours.
3. Divide chili among plates and serve.

Enjoy!

Nutrition: calories 200, fat 3, fiber 3, carbs 7, protein 8

Roasted Chicken

Preparation time: 10 minutes
Cooking time: 8 hours
Servings: 8

Ingredients:
- 1 big chicken
- 1 garlic head, peeled
- 1 yellow onion, chopped
- 1 lemon, sliced
- 1 tablespoons sweet paprika
- A pinch of sea salt
- Black pepper to the taste
- 1 teaspoon thyme, dried
- 2 carrots, chopped

Directions:
1. Stuff your chicken with half of the garlic and stuff with half of the lemon slices.
2. Rub the bird with salt, pepper, thyme and paprika both outside and inside.
3. Place carrots on the bottom of your slow cooker, add the rest of the garlic, onion and lemon slices.
4. Place the bird on top, cover and cook on Low for 8 hours.
5. Transfer chicken to a platter, carve and serve with a side salad.

Enjoy!

Nutrition: calories 200, fat 4, fiber 3, carbs 8, protein 16

Simple Italian Chicken

Preparation time: 10 minutes
Cooking time: 6 hours
Servings: 4

Ingredients:
- ¼ cup tomato paste
- 1 onion, chopped
- 2 tablespoons coconut oil
- 1 and ½ teaspoon oregano, dried
- 3 garlic cloves, minced
- ¼ teaspoon red pepper flakes
- 2 pounds mushrooms, sliced
- ½ cup chicken stock
- 10 ounces canned tomatoes, chopped
- 8 chicken thighs
- A pinch of sea salt
- Black pepper to the taste

Directions:
1. Heat up a pan with the oil over medium high heat, add onion and garlic, stir and cook for 2 minutes.
2. Transfer this to your slow cooker, add tomato paste, oregano, pepper flakes, mushrooms, tomatoes, stock, chicken pieces, some black pepper and a pinch of salt, stir well, cover and cook on Low for 6 hours.
3. Stir again, divide between plates and serve.

Enjoy!

Nutrition: calories 240, fat 4, fiber 3, carbs 8, protein 10

Wonderful Salsa Chicken

Preparation time: 10 minutes
Cooking time: 7 hours
Servings: 4

Ingredients:

- 4 chicken breasts, skinless and boneless
- ½ cup water
- 16 ounces Paleo salsa
- 1 and ½ tablespoons parsley, dried
- 1 teaspoon garlic powder
- ½ tablespoon cilantro, chopped
- 1 teaspoon onion powder
- ½ tablespoons oregano, dried
- ½ teaspoon paprika, smoked
- 1 teaspoon chili powder
- ½ teaspoon cumin, ground
- Black pepper to the taste

Directions:

1. Put the water in your slow cooker and add chicken breasts.
2. Add salsa, parsley, garlic powder, cilantro, onion powder, oregano, paprika, chili powder, cumin and black pepper to the taste.
3. Stir, cover and cook on Low for 7 hours.
4. Divide chicken on plates, drizzle the sauces on top and serve.

Enjoy!

Nutrition: calories 200, fat 4, fiber 2, carbs 7, protein 9

Superb Chicken Soup

Preparation time: 10 minutes
Cooking time: 4 hours and 10 minutes
Servings: 4

Ingredients:

- 1 jalapeno pepper, chopped
- 2 tablespoons olive oil
- 1 yellow onion, chopped
- 1 red bell pepper, chopped
- 3 garlic cloves, minced
- 4 chicken breasts, skinless and boneless
- 4 ounces canned green chilies, chopped
- 28 ounces canned tomatoes, chopped
- 2 teaspoons chili powder
- 4 cups low sodium chicken stock
- 1 teaspoon cumin, ground
- A handful cilantro, chopped
- Black pepper to the taste

Directions:

1. Heat up a pan with the oil over medium high heat, add jalapeno, onion, bell pepper and garlic, stir and sauté them for 7 minutes.
2. Transfer these to your slow cooker, add, chicken breasts, chilies, tomatoes, chili powder, stock, cumin and black pepper, stir, cover and cook on High for 4 hours.
3. Add cilantro, stir your soup, take meat out and shred using 2 forks, ladle into soup bowls, divide shredded meat in each bowl and serve.

Enjoy!

Nutrition: calories 140, fat 1, fiber 2, carbs 6, protein 7

Cashew Chicken

Preparation time: 10 minutes
Cooking time: 4 hours
Servings: 6

Ingredients:

- 1 and ½ pound chicken breast, boneless, skinless and cubed
- 1 tablespoon coconut oil
- 3 tablespoons coconut aminos
- 2 tablespoons tapioca flour
- Black pepper to the taste
- 1 tablespoon unsweetened ketchup
- 2 tablespoons white vinegar
- 1 teaspoon ginger, grated
- 2 tablespoons palm sugar
- ½ cup cashews, chopped
- 2 garlic cloves, minced
- 1 green onion, chopped

Directions:

1. Put chicken pieces in a bowl, season with black pepper, add tapioca flour and toss well.
2. Heat up a pan with the oil over medium high heat, add chicken, cook for 5 minutes and transfer to your slow cooker.
3. Add aminos, ketchup, vinegar, ginger, palm sugar and garlic, stir well, cover and cook on Low for 4 hours.
4. Add cashews and green onion, stir, divide into bowls and serve.

Enjoy!

Nutrition: calories 200, fat 3, fiber 2, carbs 8, protein 12

Chicken Stew

Preparation time: 10 minutes
Cooking time: 8 hours
Servings: 4

Ingredients:

- 1 yellow onion, chopped
- 2 pounds chicken breasts, skinless and boneless
- 4 ounces canned jalapenos, chopped
- 1 green bell pepper, chopped
- 4 ounces canned green chilies, chopped
- 7 ounces tomato sauce
- 14 ounces canned tomatoes, chopped
- 2 tablespoons coconut oil
- 3 garlic cloves, minced
- 1 tablespoon chili powder
- 1 tablespoon cumin, ground
- 2 teaspoons oregano, dried
- A bunch of cilantro, chopped
- A pinch of sea salt
- Black pepper to the taste
- 1 avocado, pitted, peeled and sliced

Directions:

1. Put the oil in your slow cooker.
2. Add onion, chicken breasts, jalapenos, bell pepper, green chilies, tomato sauce, tomatoes, garlic, chili powder, cumin, oregano, a pinch of salt and black pepper, stir, cover and cook on Low for 8 hours.
3. Add cilantro, shred chicken breasts using 2 forks, return them to the pot, stir your stew one more time, divide into bowls and top with avocado slices.

Enjoy!

Nutrition: calories 245, fat 4, fiber 5, carbs 9, protein 16

Indian Chicken Dish

Preparation time: 10 minutes
Cooking time: 6 hours
Servings: 6

Ingredients:

- 2 cups tomato puree
- ½ cup cashews, chopped, soaked for a couple of hours and drained
- ¼ cup water
- 2 and ½ pounds chicken thighs, skinless, boneless and cubed
- 2 and ½ tablespoons garam masala
- 2 garlic cloves, minced
- ½ yellow onion, chopped
- 1 teaspoon ginger powder
- A pinch of sea salt
- A pinch of cayenne pepper
- ½ teaspoon sweet paprika
- ½ cup cilantro, chopped

Directions:

1. Put the tomato puree in your slow cooker.
2. Add chicken pieces, garlic, garam masala, onion, ginger powder, a pinch of salt, cayenne pepper and paprika.
3. Stir, cover and cook on Low for 6 hours.
4. Meanwhile, in your blender, mix cashews with the water and pulse really well.
5. Add this to your chicken, stir well, divide into bowls and sprinkle cilantro on top.

Enjoy!

Nutrition: calories 189, fat 3, fiber 3, carbs 7, protein 14

Delicious Turkey Breast

Preparation time: 10 minutes
Cooking time: 8 hours
Servings: 4

Ingredients:

- 3 pounds turkey breast, bone in
- 1 cup black figs
- 3 sweet potatoes, cut into wedges
- ½ cup dried cherries, pitted
- 2 white onions, cut into wedges
- ½ cup dried cranberries
- 1/3 cup water
- 1 teaspoon onion powder
- 1 teaspoon garlic powder
- 1 teaspoon parsley flakes
- 1 teaspoon thyme, dried
- 1 teaspoon sage, dried
- 1 teaspoon paprika, dried
- A pinch of sea salt
- Black pepper to the taste

Directions:

1. Put the turkey breast in your slow cooker.
2. Add sweet potatoes, figs, cherries, onions, cranberries and water.
3. Also add parsley, garlic and onion powder, thyme, sage, paprika, salt and pepper.
4. Stir everything around the pot, cover and cook on Low for 8 hours.
5. Discard bone from turkey breast, slice meat and divide between plates.
6. Serve with the veggies, figs, cherries and berries on the side.

Enjoy!

Nutrition: calories 220, fat 5, fiber 4, carbs 8, protein 15

Thai Chicken Soup

Preparation time: 10 minutes
Cooking time: 4 hours
Servings: 6

Ingredients:

- 14 ounces canned coconut milk
- 1 butternut squash, peeled and cubed
- 1 yellow onion, chopped
- 2 cups veggie stock
- 1 tablespoon Thai chili sauce
- 1 and ½ tablespoons red curry paste
- 1 tablespoon ginger, grated
- A pinch of sea salt
- 1 pound chicken breast, skinless and boneless
- 2 garlic cloves, minced
- 2 red bell peppers, chopped
- Juice from 1 lime
- ½ cup cilantro, chopped

Directions:

1. But the coconut milk in your slow cooker.
2. Add squash pieces, onion, stock, Thai chili sauce, curry paste, ginger, a pinch of salt and garlic and stir really well.
3. Add chicken breasts, toss to coat and cook on High for 4 hours.
4. Add lime juice, stir soup, divide it into bowls, top with chopped parsley and bell peppers and serve right away.

Enjoy!

Nutrition: calories 276, fat 5, fiber 2, carbs 8, protein 16

Unbelievable Turkey Chili

Preparation time: 10 minutes
Cooking time: 4 hours
Servings: 8

Ingredients:

- 1 red bell pepper, chopped
- 2 pound turkey meat ground
- 28 ounces canned tomatoes, chopped
- 1 red onion, chopped
- 1 green bell pepper, chopped
- 4 tablespoons tomato paste
- 1 tablespoon oregano, dried
- 3 tablespoon chili powder
- 3 tablespoons cumin, ground
- A pinch of sea salt
- Black pepper to the taste

Directions:

1. Heat up a pan over medium high heat, add turkey meat, brown it for a few minutes and transfer to your slow cooker.
2. Add red and green bell pepper, onion, tomatoes, tomato paste, chili powder, oregano, cumin, a pinch of salt and black pepper to the taste, stir, cover and cook on High for 4 hours.
3. Divide into bowls and serve.

Enjoy!

Nutrition: calories 200, fat 6, fiber 4, carbs 8, protein 18

Turkey Breast And Sweet Potatoes

Preparation time: 10 minutes
Cooking time: 8 hours
Servings: 4

Ingredients:

- 3 pounds turkey breast, skinless and boneless
- 1 cup cranberries, chopped
- 2 sweet potatoes, chopped
- ½ cup raisins
- ½ cup walnuts, chopped
- 1 sweet onion, chopped
- 2 tablespoons limon juice
- 1 cup coconut sugar
- 1 teaspoon ginger, grated
- ½ teaspoon nutmeg, ground
- 1 teaspoon cinnamon powder
- ½ cup veggie stock
- 1 teaspoon poultry seasoning
- Black pepper to the taste
- 3 tablespoons olive oil

Directions:

1. Heat up a pan with the oil over medium high heat, add cranberries, walnuts, raisins, onion, lemon juice, sugar, ginger, nutmeg, cinnamon, stock and black pepper, stir well and bring to a simmer.
2. Place turkey breast in your slow cooker and add sweet potatoes next to it.
3. Add cranberries mix and poultry seasoning, toss a bit, cover and cook on Low for 8 hours.
4. Slice turkey breast and divide on plates next to sweet potatoes.
5. Drizzle the sauce from the cooker all over and serve.

Enjoy!

Nutrition: calories 264, fat 4, fiber 6, carbs 8, protein 15

Palestinian Chicken

Preparation time: 10 minutes
Cooking time: 6 hours and 5 minutes
Servings: 6

Ingredients:

- 2 and ½ pounds chicken thighs, skinless and boneless
- 1 and ½ tablespoon olive oil
- 2 yellow onions, chopped
- 1 teaspoon cinnamon powder
- ¼ teaspoon cloves, ground
- ¼ teaspoon allspice, ground
- A pinch of sea salt
- Black pepper to the taste
- A pinch of saffron
- A handful pine nuts for serving
- A handful mint, chopped for serving

Directions:

1. In a bowl, mix oil with onions, cinnamon, allspice, salt, pepper and saffron, whisk and introduce in the microwave for 5 minutes.
2. Stir again and transfer to your slow cooker.
3. Add the chicken, toss well, cover and cook on Low for 6 hours.
4. Sprinkle pine nuts and mint on top before serving,

Enjoy!

Nutrition: calories 223, fat 3, fiber 2, carbs 6, protein 13

Chicken And Sausage Delight

Preparation time: 10 minutes
Cooking time: 5 hours
Servings: 4

Ingredients:

- 4 chicken breasts, skinless and boneless
- 6 Italian sausages, sliced
- 5 garlic cloves, minced
- 1 white onion, chopped
- 1 teaspoon Italian seasoning
- A drizzle of olive oil
- 1 teaspoon garlic powder
- 29 ounces canned tomatoes, chopped
- 15 ounces tomato sauce
- 1 cup water
- ½ cup balsamic vinegar

Directions:

1. Put chicken and sausage slices in your slow cooker.
2. Add garlic, onion, Italian seasoning and the oil and toss everything.
3. Also add tomatoes, tomato sauce, garlic powder, water and the vinegar, cover and cook on High for 5 hours.
4. Stir chicken and sausage mix again, divide between plates and serve.

Enjoy!

Nutrition: calories 267, fat 4, fiber 3, carbs 7, protein 13

Savory Chicken

Preparation time: 10 minutes
Cooking time: 6 hours
Servings: 4

Ingredients:

- 2 red bell peppers, chopped
- 2 pounds chicken breasts, skinless and boneless
- 4 garlic cloves, minced
- 1 yellow onion, chopped
- 2 teaspoons paprika
- 1 cup low sodium chicken stock
- 2 teaspoons cinnamon powder
- ¼ teaspoon nutmeg, ground

Directions:

1. In a bowl, mix bell peppers with chicken breasts, garlic, onion, paprika, cinnamon and nutmeg and toss to coat.
2. Transfer everything to your slow cooker, add stock, cover and cook on Low for 6 hours.
3. Divide chicken and veggies between plates and serve.

Enjoy!

Nutrition: calories 150, fat 3, fiber 5, carbs 7, protein 10

Delicious Stuffed Chicken Breasts

Preparation time: 10 minutes
Cooking time: 6 hours
Servings: 4

Ingredients:

- 4 chicken breasts, skinless and boneless
- 1 tablespoon olive oil
- 1 small yellow onion, chopped
- 2 chili peppers, chopped
- 1 small red bell pepper, chopped
- 2 teaspoons garlic, minced
- 6 ounces spinach
- 1 and ½ teaspoon oregano, chopped
- 1 tablespoon lemon juice
- 1 cup veggie stock
- A pinch of sea salt
- Black pepper to the taste
- A handful parsley, chopped

Directions:

1. Heat up a pan with the oil over medium high heat, add bell pepper, chili peppers and onions, stir and cook for 3 minutes.
2. Add spinach and garlic, stir and cook for a couple more seconds.
3. Add a pinch of salt, black pepper and oregano, stir and take off heat.
4. Cut a pocket in each chicken breast and stuff with spinach mixture.
5. Arrange stuffed chicken breasts in your slow cooker, add stock, cover and cook on Low for 6 hours.
6. Divide on plates, sprinkle parsley on top, drizzle the lemon juice and serve.

Enjoy!

Nutrition: calories 245, fat 4, fiber 3, carbs 8, protein 15

Divine Turkey Breast

Preparation time: 10 minutes
Cooking time: 6 hours
Servings: 6

Ingredients:

- 6-pound turkey breast, skin and bone in
- 4 cups cranberries, rinsed
- 3 apples, peeled, cored and sliced
- ½ cup balsamic vinegar
- ½ cup maple syrup
- A pinch of sea salt
- Black pepper to the taste

Directions:

1. Put the turkey breast in your slow cooker.
2. Add cranberries, apple slices, a pinch of salt, black pepper, vinegar and maple syrup.
3. Toss a bit, cover and cook on Low for 6 hours.
4. Slice turkey breast and divide on plates, mash cranberries and apples a bit and add them on top of the meat.
5. Serve right away.

Enjoy!

Nutrition: calories 360, fat 4, fiber 3, carbs 9, protein 20

Tasty Kimchi Chicken

Preparation time: 10 minutes
Cooking time: 5 hours and 20 minutes
Servings: 6

Ingredients:

- 6 garlic cloves, minced
- 4 scallions, sliced
- 1 cup veggie stock
- 1 tablespoon sesame oil
- 2 teaspoons palm sugar
- 1 tablespoon coconut aminos
- 1 teaspoon ginger, minced
- 2 pounds chicken thighs, skinless and boneless
- 2 cups cabbage Kimchi

Directions:

1. In your slow cooker, mix stock with oil, scallions, garlic, sugar, aminos and ginger and whisk really well.
2. Add chicken, stir, cover and cook on Low for 5 hours.
3. Transfer chicken to plates, add Kimchi to your slow cooker, cover and cook on High for 20 minutes more.
4. Add Kimchi mix to plates next to the chicken and serve.

Enjoy!

Nutrition: Calories 240, fat 3, fiber 4, carbs 7, protein 10

Wonderful Chicken

Preparation time: 10 minutes
Cooking time: 6 hours
Servings: 6

Ingredients:

- 1 whole chicken
- 5 thyme springs, chopped
- 2 celery stalks, chopped
- 3 garlic cloves, minced
- 2 carrots, chopped
- 1 yellow onion, chopped
- A pinch of white pepper
- Juice of 1 lemon

Directions:

1. Put half of the thyme, garlic, celery, onion and carrots in your slow cooker.
2. Add the chicken on top and season with a pinch of white pepper.
3. Add the rest of the thyme, onion, garlic, celery and carrots on top, drizzle the lemon juice, cover and cook on Low for 6 hours.
4. Divide chicken between plates and serve.

Enjoy!

Nutrition: calories 230, fat 4, fiber 2, carbs 6, protein 6

Tasty Greek Chicken

Preparation time: 10 minutes
Cooking time: 4 hours
Servings: 4

Ingredients:

- 1 and ½ pounds chicken breast, skinless and boneless
- Juice from 2 lemons
- 1 rosemary spring, chopped
- ¼ cup olive oil
- 3 garlic cloves, minced
- A pinch of salt and black pepper
- 1 cucumber, chopped
- 1 cup kalamata olives, pitted and sliced
- ¼ cup red onions, chopped
- 2 tablespoons red vinegar

Directions:

1. In your slow cooker, mix chicken with lemon juice, rosemary, oil, garlic, salt and pepper, stir, cover and cook on High for 4 hours.
2. Transfer chicken to a cutting board, shred with 2 forks, and transfer to a bowl, add cucumber, olives, onion and vinegar, toss, divide between plates and serve.

Enjoy!

Nutrition: calories 200, fat 3, fiber 3, carbs 12, protein 3

Mexican Chicken

Preparation time: 10 minutes
Cooking time: 4 hours
Servings: 8

Ingredients:

- 4 pounds chicken breast, skinless and boneless
- 1 cup chicken stock
- 1 yellow onion, chopped
- 1 tablespoon chipotle powder
- 4 garlic cloves, minced
- 2 teaspoons cumin, ground
- A pinch of salt and black pepper
- 1 teaspoon chili powder
- Lime wedges, for serving

Directions:

1. In your slow cooker, mix chicken with stock, onion, chipotle powder, garlic, cumin, salt, pepper and chili, stir, cover and cook on High for 4 hours.
2. Transfer chicken to a cutting board, cool down, slice, divide between plates and serve with cooking juices on top, with a side salad and lemon wedges.

Enjoy!

Nutrition: calories 271, fat 3, fiber 6, carbs 9, protein 8

Chicken Chowder

Preparation time: 10 minutes
Cooking time: 6 hours
Servings: 4

Ingredients:
- 3 chicken breasts, skinless and boneless and cubed
- 4 cups chicken stock
- 1 sweet potato, cubed
- 8 ounces canned green chilies, chopped
- 1 yellow onion, chopped
- 15 ounces coconut cream
- 1 teaspoon garlic powder
- 4 bacon strips, cooked and crumbled
- A pinch of salt and black pepper
- 1 tablespoon parsley, chopped

Directions:
1. In your slow cooker, mix chicken with stock, sweet potato, green chilies, onion, garlic powder, salt and pepper, stir, cover and cook on Low for 5 hours and 40 minutes.
2. Add coconut cream and parsley, stir, cover and cook on Low for 20 minutes more.
3. Ladle chowder into bowls, sprinkle bacon on top and serve.

Enjoy!

Nutrition: calories 232, fat 3, fiber 7, carbs 14, protein 7

Flavored Chicken Soup

Preparation time: 10 minutes
Cooking time: 4 hours
Servings: 4

Ingredients:
- 1 pound chicken breast, skinless, boneless and cubed
- 15 ounces canned tomatoes and chilies, chopped
- 2 teaspoons cumin, ground
- A pinch of salt and black pepper
- 1 yellow onion, chopped
- 1 chipotle chili in adobo sauce
- ½ teaspoon oregano, dried
- 1 red bell pepper, chopped
- 2 cup chicken stock
- 1 avocado, pitted, peeled and chopped
- ½ cup cilantro, chopped

Directions:
1. In your slow cooker, mix chicken with tomatoes and chilies, cumin, salt, pepper, onion, chipotle chili, oregano, bell pepper and stock, stir, cover and cook on Low for 4 hours.
2. Add cilantro, stir, ladle into bowls and serve with avocado on top.

Enjoy!

Nutrition: calories 300, fat 3, fiber 7, carbs 16, protein 4

Chicken and Olives

Preparation time: 10 minutes
Cooking time: 6 hours
Servings: 6

Ingredients:

- 2 pounds chicken thighs, boneless and skinless
- 1 yellow onion, chopped
- 3 carrots, chopped
- 1/3 cup prunes, dried and halved
- 3 garlic cloves, minced
- ½ cup green olives, pitted
- 2 teaspoon sweet paprika
- 1 teaspoon cinnamon, ground
- 2 teaspoons cumin, ground
- 2 teaspoons ginger, grated
- 1 cup chicken stock
- A pinch of salt and black pepper
- 1 tablespoon cilantro, chopped

Directions:

1. In your slow cooker, mix chicken with onion, carrots, prunes, garlic, olives, paprika, cinnamon, cumin, ginger, stock, salt and pepper, stir, cover and cook on Low for 6 hours.
2. Divide on plates, sprinkle cilantro on top and serve.

Enjoy!

Nutrition: calories 384, fat 12, fiber 4, carbs 20, protein 34

Italian Chicken

Preparation time: 10 minutes
Cooking time: 6 hours
Servings: 4

Ingredients:

- 4 chicken thighs, skinless and boneless
- 15 ounces canned tomatoes, chopped
- ½ cup mushrooms, sliced
- ½ cup kalamata olives, pitted
- 2 teaspoons Italian seasoning
- 3 garlic cloves, minced
- A pinch of salt and black pepper
- 2 cups chicken stock
- 2 cups baby spinach
- 12 ounces tomato paste
- Cooking spray

Directions:

1. Grease your slow cooker with cooking spray and add chicken, tomatoes, mushrooms, olives, Italian seasoning, garlic, salt, pepper, and stock and tomato paste.
2. Stir, cover, cook on Low for 6 hours, add spinach, stir, leave everything aside for 10 minutes, divide between plates and serve.

Enjoy!

Nutrition: calories 321, fat 4, fiber 7, carbs 16, protein 14

Pineapple Chicken

Preparation time: 10 minutes
Cooking time: 7 hours
Servings: 8

Ingredients:
- 8 chicken thighs, bone in
- A pinch of salt and black pepper
- 2 tablespoon ghee
- 1 cup pineapple juice
- ½ cup chicken stock
- 2 tablespoons coconut sugar
- 3 tablespoons coconut aminos
- 2 tablespoon apple cider vinegar
- ½ teaspoon ginger, grated
- 1 teaspoon garlic powder
- 8 ounces canned pineapple chunks
- 8 ounces canned pineapple, crushed
- 1 red bell pepper, chopped
- 1 red onion, chopped
- 2 tablespoons parsley, chopped
- ½ teaspoon sesame seeds

Directions:
1. In your slow cooker, mix chicken with salt, pepper, ghee, pineapple juice, stock, coconut sugar, aminos, vinegar, ginger, garlic powder, pineapple chunks and crushed pineapple, red bell pepper and onion, stir, cover and cook on Low for 7 hours.
2. Add parsley and sesame seeds, toss, divide between plates and serve.

Enjoy!

Nutrition: calories 321, fat 5, fiber 7, carbs 15, protein 4

Lemon and Garlic Chicken

Preparation time: 10 minutes
Cooking time: 4 hours
Servings: 6

Ingredients:
- 1 yellow onion, cut into quarters
- ¼ cup olive oil
- 1 pound carrots, sliced
- 6 chicken thighs, bone in
- 3 tablespoons lemon juice
- 4 garlic cloves, minced
- 1 lemon, sliced
- 3 rosemary sprigs, chopped
- 6 thyme sprigs, chopped
- A pinch of salt and black pepper

Directions:
1. In your slow cooker, mix onion with oil, carrots, chicken, lemon juice, garlic, lemon slices, rosemary, thyme, salt and pepper, stir, cover and cook on High for 4 hours.
2. Divide between plates and serve.

Enjoy!

Nutrition: calories 300, fat 6, fiber 5, carbs 15, protein 5

Creamy Chicken

Preparation time: 10 minutes
Cooking time: 4 hours
Servings: 8

Ingredients:

- 2 pounds chicken breasts, skinless and boneless
- 2 tablespoons water
- 1 tablespoon olive oil
- 1 and ½ teaspoons cumin, ground
- 1 teaspoon chili powder
- 1 teaspoon garlic powder
- 1 teaspoon onion powder
- ½ teaspoon smoked paprika
- ½ teaspoon oregano, dried
- A pinch of salt and black pepper to the taste
- 8 ounces coconut cream
- Cooking spray

Directions:

1. Grease your slow cooker with cooking spray and add chicken, water, oil, cumin, chili, garlic powder, onion powder, paprika, oregano, salt and pepper, toss, cover and cook on High for 3 hours and 30 minutes.
2. Shred chicken using 2 forks, add coconut cream, toss, cover and cook on High for 30 minutes more.
3. Divide chicken mix between plates and serve.

Enjoy!

Nutrition: calories 312, fat 4, fiber 6, carbs 20, protein 5

Chicken Breasts and Peach Sauce

Preparation time: 10 minutes
Cooking time: 6 hours
Servings: 8

Ingredients:

- 6 chicken breasts, skinless and boneless
- 12 ounces orange juice
- 2 tablespoons lemon juice
- 15 ounces canned peaches and their juice
- 1 teaspoon coconut aminos

Directions:

1. In your slow cooker, mix chicken with orange juice, lemon juice, peaches and coconut aminos, toss, cover and cook on Low for 6 hours.
2. Divide chicken breasts on plates, drizzle peach and orange sauce all over and serve.

Enjoy!

Nutrition: calories 251, fat 4, fiber 6, carbs 18, protein 14

Sweet Chicken

Preparation time: 10 minutes
Cooking time: 4 hours
Servings: 4

Ingredients:
- 2 pounds chicken thighs
- Salt and black pepper to the taste
- ¾ cup sweet Bbq sauce
- A pinch of cayenne pepper
- 1 cup apple juice
- 1 teaspoon red pepper, crushed
- 2 teaspoons paprika
- ½ teaspoon basil, dried

Directions:
1. In your slow cooker, mix chicken with salt, pepper, bbq sauce, cayenne, apple juice, red pepper, paprika and basil, stir, cover and cook on High for 4 hours.
2. Divide everything into bowls and serve.

Enjoy!

Nutrition: calories 200, fat 3, fiber 6, carbs 10, protein 17

Turkey Gumbo

Preparation time: 10 minutes
Cooking time: 7 hours
Servings: 4

Ingredients:
- 1 pound turkey wings
- Salt and black pepper to the taste
- 5 ounces water
- 1 yellow onion, chopped
- 1 yellow bell pepper, chopped
- 3 garlic cloves, chopped
- 2 tablespoons chili powder
- 1 and ½ teaspoons cumin, ground
- A pinch of cayenne pepper
- 2 cups veggies stock

Directions:
1. In your slow cooker, mix turkey with salt, pepper, onion, bell pepper, garlic, chili powder, cumin, cayenne and stock, stir, cover and cook on Low for 7 hours.
2. Divide everything between plates and serve.

Enjoy!

Nutrition: calories 232, fat 4, fiber 7, carbs 17, protein 20

Ginger Duck

Preparation time: 10 minutes
Cooking time: 8 hours
Servings: 6

Ingredients:
- 1 duck, chopped into medium pieces
- 1 celery stalk, chopped
- 2 carrots, chopped
- 2 cups chicken stock
- Salt and black pepper to the taste
- 1 tablespoon ginger, grated

Directions:
1. In your slow cooker, mix duck with celery, carrots, stock, salt, pepper and ginger, stir, cover and cook on Low for 8 hours.
2. Divide duck, ginger sauce between plates, and serve.

Enjoy!

Nutrition: calories 200, fat 3, fiber 6, carbs 19, protein 17

Flavored Turkey Wings

Preparation time: 10 minutes
Cooking time: 8 hours
Servings: 4

Ingredients:
- 4 turkey wings
- 1 yellow onion, chopped
- 1 carrot, chopped
- 3 garlic cloves, minced
- 1 celery stalk, chopped
- 1 cup chicken stock
- Salt and black pepper to the taste
- 2 tablespoons olive oil
- A pinch of rosemary, dried
- 2 bay leaves
- A pinch of sage, dried
- A pinch of thyme, dried

Directions:
1. In your slow cooker, mix turkey with onion, carrot, garlic, celery, stock, salt, pepper, oil, rosemary, sage, thyme and bay leaves, toss, cover and cook on Low for 8 hours.
2. Divide between plates and serve hot.

Enjoy!

Nutrition: calories 223, fat 5, fiber 7, carbs 18, protein 14

Turkey and Orange Sauce

Preparation time: 10 minutes
Cooking time: 8 hours
Servings: 4

Ingredients:

- 4 turkey wings
- 2 tablespoons ghee, melted
- 2 tablespoons olive oil
- 1 and ½ cups cranberries, dried
- Salt and black pepper to the taste
- 1 yellow onion, roughly chopped
- 1 cup walnuts
- 1 cup orange juice
- 1 bunch thyme, chopped

Directions:

1. In your slow cooker mix ghee with oil, turkey wings, cranberries, salt, pepper, onion, walnuts, orange juice and thyme, stir a bit, cover and cook on Low for 8 hours.
2. Divide turkey and orange sauce between plates and serve.

Enjoy!

Nutrition: calories 300, fat 12, fiber 4, carbs 17, protein 1

Cinnamon Chicken

Preparation time: 10 minutes
Cooking time: 4 hours
Servings: 8

Ingredients:

- 1 whole chicken, cut into medium pieces
- 1 tablespoon olive oil
- 1 and ½ tablespoons lemon zest, grated
- 1 cup chicken stock
- 1 tablespoon thyme, chopped
- 1 teaspoon cinnamon powder
- Salt and black pepper to the taste
- 1 tablespoon cumin, ground
- 2 teaspoons garlic powder

Directions:

1. In your slow cooker, mix chicken with oil, lemon zest, stock, thyme, cinnamon, salt, pepper, cumin and garlic, stir, cover and cook on High for 4 hours.
2. Divide everything between plates and serve.

Enjoy!

Nutrition: calories 261, fat 4, fiber 6, carbs 12, protein 22

Chicken and Celery

Preparation time: 10 minutes
Cooking time: 4 hours
Servings: 4

Ingredients:

- 6 chicken thighs
- 1 teaspoon olive oil
- Salt and black pepper to the taste
- 1 yellow onion, chopped
- 3 celery stalk, chopped
- ½ teaspoon thyme, dried
- 2 tablespoons tomato paste
- 15 ounces canned tomatoes, chopped
- 2 cups chicken stock

Directions:

1. In your slow cooker, mix chicken with oil, salt, pepper, onion, celery, thyme, tomato paste, tomatoes and stock, stir, cover and cook on High for 4 hours.
2. Divide between plates and serve hot.

Enjoy!

Nutrition: calories 261, fat 10, fiber 6, carbs 17, protein 27

Chicken Stew

Preparation time: 10 minutes
Cooking time: 6 hours
Servings: 4

Ingredients:

- 1 pound smoked pork sausage, sliced
- 1 tablespoon olive oil
- 1 pound chicken thighs, halved
- Salt and black pepper to the taste
- 1 teaspoon Cajun spice
- 1 bell pepper, chopped
- 1 yellow onion, chopped
- 1 celery stalk, chopped
- 4 garlic cloves, minced
- 2 quarts chicken stock
- 15 ounces canned tomatoes, chopped
- ½ cup parsley, chopped

Directions:

1. In your slow cooker, mix smoked sausage with oil, chicken, salt, pepper, Cajun spice, bell pepper, onion, celery, garlic, stock and tomatoes, stir, cover and cook on Low for 6 hours.
2. Add parsley, stir, divide stew into bowls and serve.

Enjoy!

Nutrition: calories 223, fat 12, fiber 6, carbs 20, protein 10

French Chicken and Bacon

Preparation time: 10 minutes
Cooking time: 4 hours
Servings: 4

Ingredients:

- 2 pounds chicken thighs, skinless and boneless
- 4 ounces bacon, chopped
- ¼ cup olive oil
- 2 brown onions, sliced
- 2 garlic cloves, minced
- 14 ounces chicken stock
- 1 bay leaf
- 7 ounces white mushrooms, sliced
- 1 cup parsley, chopped
- Salt and black pepper to the taste

Directions:

1. In your slow cooker, mix chicken with bacon, oil, onion, garlic, stock, bay leaf, mushrooms, salt, pepper and parsley, stir, cover and cook on High for 4 hours.
2. Divide chicken mix into plates and serve hot.

Enjoy!

Nutrition: calories 300, fat 13, fiber 7, carbs 17, protein 18

Chicken and Sweet Potatoes

Preparation time: 10 minutes
Cooking time: 4 hours
Servings: 4

Ingredients:

- 2 sweet potatoes, cut into medium cubes
- 1 yellow onion, chopped
- 4 big tomatoes, cut into wedges
- ¼ cup chicken stock
- 8 chicken thighs, bone in
- Salt and black pepper to the taste
- 2 bay leaves

Directions:

1. In your slow cooker, mix chicken thighs with sweet potatoes, onion, tomatoes, stock, salt, pepper and bay leaves, stir a bit, cover and cook on High for 4 hours.
2. Divide between plates and serve.

Enjoy!

Nutrition: calories 300, fat 12, fiber 6, carbs 17, protein 12

Chicken and Apricot Sauce

Preparation time: 10 minutes
Cooking time: 4 hours
Servings: 4

Ingredients:

- 1 pound chicken thighs, skinless and boneless
- Salt and black pepper to the taste
- 1 tablespoon olive oil
- ½ teaspoon sweet paprika
- ½ cup veggie stock
- ½ teaspoon marjoram, dried
- 2 tablespoons white vinegar
- ¼ cup apricot preserves
- 1 and ½ teaspoon ginger, grated
- 2 tablespoons stevia

Directions:

1. In your slow cooker, mix chicken with oil, salt, pepper, paprika, stock, marjoram, vinegar, apricot preserves, ginger and stevia, toss well, cover and cook on High for 4 hours.
2. Divide between plates and serve.

Enjoy!

Nutrition: calories 251, fat 7, fiber 8, carbs 14, protein 17

Flavored Chicken Thighs

Preparation time: 10 minutes
Cooking time: 4 hours
Servings: 6

Ingredients:

- 10 chicken thighs, skinless and boneless
- 2 jalapeno peppers, chopped
- 28 ounces canned tomatoes and their juice, chopped
- 2 teaspoons cumin, ground
- 2 tablespoons ginger, chopped
- ½ cup ghee, melted
- 2 teaspoons garam masala
- Salt and black pepper to the taste
- 1 cup coconut cream
- ¼ cup cilantro, chopped

Directions:

1. In your slow cooker, mix chicken thighs with jalapenos, tomatoes, cumin, ginger, ghee, garam masala, salt, pepper and coconut cream, stir, cover and cook on High for 4 hours.
2. Add cilantro, stir, divide into bowls and serve.

Enjoy!

Nutrition: calories 300, fat 13, fiber 6, carbs 17, protein 20

Creamy Chicken and Broccoli

Preparation time: 10 minutes
Cooking time: 5 hours
Servings: 6

Ingredients:
- 2 chicken breasts, skinless and boneless
- 1 tablespoon ghee
- 1 tablespoon olive oil
- ½ cup yellow onion, chopped
- 14 ounces chicken stock
- Salt and black pepper to the taste
- A pinch of red pepper flakes
- 1 tablespoon parsley, chopped
- 3 cups broccoli florets
- 4 ounces coconut cream

Directions:
1. In your slow cooker, mix chicken with ghee, oil, onion, stock, salt, pepper, pepper flakes and broccoli, stir, cover and cook on High for 4 hours and 30 minutes.
2. Add parsley and coconut cream, toss, cover and cook on High for 30 minutes more.
3. Divide chicken and broccoli between plates and serve with the coconut sauce drizzled all over.

Enjoy!

Nutrition: calories 300, fat 7, fiber 7, carbs 26, protein 27

Creole Chicken, Sausage and Shrimp

Preparation time: 10 minutes
Cooking time: 6 hours
Servings: 4

Ingredients:
- 8 ounces shrimp, peeled and deveined
- 8 ounces sausages, sliced
- 8 ounces chicken breasts, skinless, boneless and chopped
- 2 tablespoons olive oil
- 1 teaspoon Creole seasoning
- 2 teaspoons thyme, dried
- A pinch of cayenne pepper
- A pinch of salt and black pepper
- 2 cups canned tomatoes, chopped
- 3 garlic cloves, minced
- 1 yellow onion, chopped
- 1 green bell pepper, chopped
- 3 celery stalks, chopped
- 1 cup chicken stock
- 3 tablespoons parsley, chopped

Directions:
1. In your slow cooker, mix sausages with chicken, oil, Creole seasoning, thyme, cayenne, salt, pepper, tomatoes, garlic, onion, bell pepper, celery and stock, stir, cover and cook on Low for 5 hours and 30 minutes.
2. Add shrimp, stir a bit, cover and cook on Low for 30 minutes more.
3. Divide everything into bowls and serve.

Enjoy!

Nutrition: calories 261, fat 7, fiber 7, carbs 28, protein 17

Salsa Chicken Soup

Preparation time: 10 minutes
Cooking time: 4 hours
Servings: 4

Ingredients:

- 4 chicken breasts, skinless, boneless and cubed
- 2 tablespoons olive oil
- 1 onion, chopped
- 3 garlic cloves, minced
- 16 ounces Paleo salsa
- Salt and black pepper to the taste
- 29 ounces canned tomatoes, peeled and chopped
- 29 ounces chicken stock
- 2 tablespoons parsley, chopped
- 1 teaspoon garlic powder
- 1 tablespoon onion powder
- 1 tablespoon chili powder

Directions:

1. In your slow cooker, mix chicken with oil, onion, garlic, salsa, salt, pepper, stock, tomatoes, garlic powder, onion powder and chili powder, stir, cover and cook on High for 4 hours.
2. Add parsley, stir, ladle soup into bowls and serve.

Enjoy!

Nutrition: calories 231, fat 6, fiber 7, carbs 18, protein 19

Paleo Slow Cooker Meat Recipes

Hearty Pork Ribs

Preparation time: 12 hours and 10 minutes
Cooking time: 6 hours
Servings: 4

Ingredients:
- 4 cups vinegar
- 4 pounds pork ribs
- 2 tablespoons apple cider vinegar
- 2 cups water
- 3 tablespoons coconut aminos
- Black pepper to the taste
- A pinch of garlic powder
- A pinch of Chinese 5 spice

Directions:
1. Put your ribs in a big bowl, add white vinegar and water, toss, cover and keep in the fridge for 12 hours.
2. Drain ribs, season with black pepper to the taste, garlic powder and Chinese 5 spice and rub well.
3. Place ribs in your slow cooker and add apple cider vinegar and aminos as well.
4. Toss to coat well, cover slow cooker and cook on High for 6 hours.
5. Divide ribs between plates and serve.

Enjoy!

Nutrition: calories 300, fat 6, fiber 3, carbs 8, protein 15

Simple And Easy Roast

Preparation time: 10 minutes
Cooking time: 8 hours and 30 minutes
Servings: 6

Ingredients:
- 4 pounds beef chuck roast
- 1 cup veggie stock
- 1 tablespoon coconut oil
- 1 bay leaf
- 10 thyme springs
- 4 garlic cloves, minced
- 1 carrot, roughly chopped
- 2 celery ribs, roughly chopped
- 1 cauliflower head, florets separated
- A pinch of sea salt
- Black pepper to the taste
- 1 onion, roughly chopped

Directions:
1. Season beef with a pinch of sea salt and some black pepper.
2. Heat up a pan with the oil over medium high heat, add beef roast, brown for 5 minutes on each side and then transfer to your slow cooker.
3. Add thyme springs, stock, bay leaf, garlic, celery, onion and carrot, cover and cook on Low for 8 hours.
4. Add cauliflower, cover slow cooker again and cook on High for 20 minutes more.
5. Divide roast and veggies between plates and serve.

Enjoy!

Nutrition: calories 340, fat 5, fiber 3, carbs 8, protein 22

Mexican Pork Delight

Preparation time: 10 minutes
Cooking time: 8 hours
Servings: 6

Ingredients:
- 1 yellow onion, chopped
- 2 tablespoons sweet paprika
- 15 ounces canned tomato, roasted and chopped
- 1 teaspoon cumin, ground
- 1 teaspoon coconut oil
- A pinch of sea salt
- Black pepper to the taste
- A pinch of nutmeg, ground
- 5 pounds pork roast
- Juice of 1 lemon
- ¼ cup apple cider vinegar

Directions:
1. Heat up a pan with the oil over medium high heat, add onions, stir and brown them for a couple of minutes.
2. Transfer onions to your slow cooker, add paprika, tomato, cumin, nutmeg, lemon juice, vinegar, a pinch of salt and black pepper and whisk really well.
3. Add pork, toss to coat and cook on Low for 8 hours.
4. Slice roast, arrange on plates and serve with tomatoes and onions mix.

Enjoy!

Nutrition: calories 350, fat 5, fiber 2, carbs 8, protein 24

Hawaiian Pork

Preparation time: 10 minutes
Cooking time: 6 hours
Servings: 4

Ingredients:
- 2 pounds pork chops
- 1/3 cup coconut sugar
- ¼ cup sugar free ketchup
- 15 ounces pineapple, cubed
- 3 tablespoons apple cider vinegar
- 5 tablespoons coconut aminos
- 2 teaspoons garlic, minced
- 3 tablespoons tapioca flour
- Cilantro, chopped for serving

Directions:
1. In a bowl, mix ketchup with sugar, vinegar, aminos and tapioca and whisk well.
2. Add pork chops, toss well and transfer everything to your slow cooker.
3. Add pineapple and garlic, toss again, cover and cook on Low for 6 hours.
4. Sprinkle cilantro, stir gently, divide everything between plates and serve.

Enjoy!

Nutrition: calories 345, fat 5, fiber 6, carbs 7, protein 14

Incredible Pork Tenderloin

Preparation time: 10 minutes
Cooking time: 8 hours
Servings: 4

Ingredients:

- A pinch of nutmeg, ground
- 2 pounds pork tenderloin
- 4 apples, cored and sliced
- 2 tablespoons maple syrup

Directions:

1. Place half of the apples in your Crockpot and sprinkle nutmeg over them.
2. Add pork tenderloin, top with the rest of the apples, sprinkle some more nutmeg and drizzle the maple syrup.
3. Cover and cook on Low for 8 hours.
4. Slice pork tenderloin, divide it between plates and serve with apple slices and cooking juices on top.

Enjoy!

Nutrition: calories 400, fat 4, fiber 5, carbs 8, protein 20

Super Easy Pork Dinner

Preparation time: 10 minutes
Cooking time: 4 hours
Servings: 8

Ingredients:

- 1 pound chorizo, ground
- 1 pound pork, ground
- 3 tablespoons olive oil
- 1 tomato, chopped
- 1 avocado, pitted, peeled and chopped
- Black pepper to the taste
- 1 small red onion, chopped
- 2 tablespoons Paleo enchilada sauce
- Scrambled eggs for serving

Directions:

1. Heat up a pan with the oil over medium high heat, add pork meat, stir, brown for a couple of minutes and transfer to your slow cooker.
2. Add salt, pepper, chorizo, onion and enchilada sauce, stir, cover and cook on Low for 4 hours.
3. Divide between plates and serve with chopped tomato, avocado and maybe with some scrambled eggs on top.

Enjoy!

Nutrition: calories 300, fat 12, fiber 3, carbs 7, protein 17

Simple Pork Stew

Preparation time: 10 minutes
Cooking time: 8 hours
Servings: 6

Ingredients:

- 1 tablespoon olive oil
- 2 pounds pork loin, cubed
- 1 cup tapioca flour
- 3 garlic cloves, minced
- 6 baby carrots, halved
- 2 onions, chopped
- Black pepper to the taste
- A pinch of sea salt
- 1 cabbage head, shredded
- 3 cups veggie stock
- 28 ounces canned tomatoes, chopped
- 3 big sweet potatoes, cubed

Directions:

1. Put pork in a bowl, add tapioca flour and toss well.
2. Heat up a pan with the oil over medium high heat, add meat, brown for a few minutes on each side and place in your slow cooker.
3. Add a pinch of salt, black pepper, carrots, garlic, onion, potatoes, cabbage, stock and tomatoes, stir well, cover and cook on Low for 8 hours.
4. Divide stew into bowls and serve right away.

Enjoy!

Nutrition: calories 300, fat 5, fiber 4, carbs 8, protein 15

Simple Beef Stew

Preparation time: 10 minutes
Cooking time: 8 hours
Servings: 6

Ingredients:

- 2 pound beef, cubed
- 2 tablespoons Moroccan spices
- 2 big white onions, chopped
- Black pepper to the taste
- 2 cups veggie stock
- 1/3 cup coconut oil, melted
- 1 lemon, sliced
- 3 garlic cloves, minced
- Zest from 1 lemon, grated
- Juice from 2 limes
- 1 bunch cilantro, chopped
- 1 butternut squash, peeled and cubed

Directions:

1. Put the stock in your slow cooker, add beef, spices, onions, black pepper, garlic, lemon slices, lemon zest, lime juice and oil.
2. Stir everything to coat well, cover and cook on Low for 7 hours.
   Add cilantro and squash, stir, cover and cook for 1 more hour on Low.
3. Divide into serving bowls and serve right away.

Enjoy!

Nutrition: calories 320, fat 10, fiber 3, carbs 5, protein 15

Lamb Stew

Preparation time: 10 minutes
Cooking time: 8 hours
Servings: 4

Ingredients:
- 1 and ½ pounds lamb meat, cubed
- ¼ cup tapioca flour
- Black pepper to the taste
- A pinch of sea salt
- 2 tablespoons olive oil
- 1 teaspoon rosemary, dried
- 1 onion, sliced
- ½ teaspoon thyme, dried
- 2 cups water
- 1 cup baby carrots
- 2 cups sweet potatoes, chopped

Directions:
1. In a bowl, mix lamb with tapioca and toss to coat.
2. Heat up a pan with the oil over medium high heat, add meat, brown it on all sides and transfer to your slow cooker.
3. Heat up the pan again over medium high heat, add onion, stir, cook for 3 minutes and add to your slow cooker as well.
4. Also add a pinch of salt, pepper, rosemary, thyme, water, carrots and sweet potatoes, stir, cover and cook on Low for 8 hours.
5. Divide lamb stew between plates and serve hot.

Enjoy!

Nutrition: calories 350, fat 8, fiber 3, carbs 6, protein 16

Flavored Lamb Leg

Preparation time: 10 minutes
Cooking time: 8 hours
Servings: 4

Ingredients:
- 2 tablespoons olive oil
- 1 lamb leg, bone in
- 1 garlic head, peeled and cloves separated
- 5 sweet potatoes, cubed
- 5 rosemary springs
- 2 cups low sodium chicken stock
- A pinch of sea salt
- Black pepper to the taste

Directions:
1. Rub your lamb leg with the oil, a pinch of salt and some black pepper.
2. Place the potatoes and the garlic cloves on the bottom of your slow cooker.
3. Add lamb leg, rosemary springs and stock.
4. Cover the slow cooker and cook lamb on Low for 8 hours.
5. Divide lamb and potatoes between plates and serve.

Enjoy!

Nutrition: calories 350, fat 6, fiber 5, carbs 8, protein 12

Exotic Lamb Curry

Preparation time: 10 minutes
Cooking time: 4 hours
Servings: 4

Ingredients:

- 1 and ½ tablespoons sweet paprika
- 3 tablespoons curry powder
- Black pepper to the taste
- A pinch of sea salt
- 2 pounds lamb meat, cubed
- 2 tablespoons coconut oil
- 3 carrots, chopped
- 4 celery stalks, chopped
- 1 onion, chopped
- 4 celery stalks, chopped
- 1 cup low sodium chicken stock
- 4 garlic cloves minced
- 1 cup coconut milk

Directions:

1. Heat up a pan with the oil over medium high heat, add lamb meat, brown it on all sides and transfer to your slow cooker.
2. Heat up the pan again over medium high heat, add stock, stir, heat it up and add to the slow cooker as well.
3. Add onions, celery and carrots to the slow cooker and stir everything gently.
4. In a bowl, mix paprika with a pinch of salt, black pepper and curry powder and stir.
5. Add spice mix to the cooker and toss everything.
6. Add coconut milk, cover and cook on High for 4 hours.
7. Divide into bowls and serve.

Nutrition: calories 300, fat 4, fiber 4, carbs 8, protein 13

Tasty Lamb Shanks

Preparation time: 10 minutes
Cooking time: 8 hours and 20 minutes
Servings: 4

Ingredients:

- 4 lamb shanks, trimmed
- 3 tablespoons coconut oil
- ¼ cup arrowroot flour
- 1 onion, chopped
- 2 carrots, chopped
- 15 ounces canned tomatoes, chopped
- 2 garlic cloves, minced
- 2 celery stalks, chopped
- 2 tablespoons tomato paste
- 2 cups veggie stock
- 1 tablespoon rosemary, dried
- 1 tablespoon thyme, dried
- 1 tablespoon oregano, dried
- Black pepper to the taste
- A pinch of sea salt

Directions:

1. Heat up a pan with 2 tablespoons oil over medium high heat, add lamb shanks, brown them for 5 minutes on each side and transfer to your slow cooker.
2. Heat up the pan again with the rest of the oil over medium heat, add carrot, celery, garlic and onion, stir and cook for 8 minutes.
3. Add tomato paste, tomatoes, stock, a pinch of salt, black pepper, thyme, rosemary and oregano, stir, cook for 1 minute and pour over lamb shanks.
4. Cover your slow cooker and cook on Low for 7 hours.
5. Divide lamb shanks between plates, stir veggies and sauce left in the slow cooker, cover again and cook on High for 1 more hour.
6. Pour over lamb shanks and serve.

Enjoy!

Nutrition: calories 350, fat 5, fiber 4, carbs 9, protein 20

Lamb And Bacon Stew

Preparation time: 10 minutes
Cooking time: 7 hours and 10 minutes
Servings: 6

Ingredients:

- 2 tablespoons tapioca flour
- 2 ounces bacon, cooked and crumbled
- 1 and ½ pounds lamb loin, chopped
- Black pepper to the taste
- A pinch of sea salt
- 1 garlic clove, minced
- 1 cup yellow onion, chopped
- 3 and ½ cups veggie stock
- 1 cup carrots, chopped
- 1 cup celery, chopped
- 2 cups sweet potatoes, chopped
- 1 tablespoon thyme, chopped
- 1 bay leaf
- 2 tablespoons coconut oil

Directions:

1. Put lamb meat in a bowl, add tapioca, a pinch of salt and pepper and toss to coat.
2. Heat up a pan with the oil over medium high heat, add lamb, brown for 5 minutes on each side and transfer to your slow cooker.
3. Heat up the pan again over medium heat, add onion and garlic, stir, sauté for 4 minutes and add to slow cooker.
4. Add bacon, carrots, potatoes, bay leaf, stock, thyme and celery to the slow cooker as well, stir gently, cover and cook on Low for 7 hours.
5. Discard bay leaf, stir your stew, divide into bowls and serve.

Enjoy!

Nutrition: calories 360, fat 5, fiber 3, carbs 8, protein 16

Amazing Mediterranean Pork

Preparation time: 20 hours and 10 minutes
Cooking time: 8 hours
Servings: 6

Ingredients:

- 3 pounds pork shoulder, boneless

For the marinade:

- ¼ cup olive oil
- 2 teaspoons oregano, dried
- ¼ cup lemon juice
- 2 teaspoons mustard
- 2 teaspoons mint
- 6 garlic cloves, minced
- 2 teaspoons Paleo pesto sauce
- Black pepper to the taste
- A pinch of sea salt

Directions:

1. In a bowl, mix oil with lemon juice, oregano, mint, mustard, garlic, pesto, salt and pepper and stir very well.
2. Rub pork shoulder with the marinade, cover and keep in the fridge for 10 hours.
3. Flip pork shoulder and keep in the fridge for 10 more hours.
4. Transfer to your slow cooker along with the marinade, cover and cook on Low for 8 hours.
5. Slice roast and serve with a tasty side salad!

Enjoy!

Nutrition: calories 300, fat 4, fiber 6, carbs 7, protein 10

Special Roast

Preparation time: 10 minutes
Cooking time: 4 hours
Servings: 6

Ingredients:

- 1 pound sweet potatoes, chopped
- 3 and ½ pounds pork roast
- 8 medium carrots, chopped
- 15 ounces canned tomatoes, chopped
- 1 yellow onion, chopped
- Grated zest and juice from 1 lemon
- 4 garlic cloves, minced
- 3 bay leaves
- Black pepper to the taste
- ½ cup kalamata olives, pitted
- A pinch of salt

Directions:

1. Put potatoes in your slow cooker and mix with carrots, tomatoes, onions, lemon juice and zest.
2. Also add pork, bay leaves, a pinch of salt, black pepper and garlic, stir, cover and cook on High for 4 hours.
3. Transfer meat to a cutting board, slice it and divide among plates.
4. Discard bay leaves, transfer veggies to a bowl, mash them, mix with olives and add next to the meat.
5. Serve right away!

Enjoy!

Nutrition: calories 250, fat 4, fiber 3, carbs 8, protein 13

Delicious Beef And Pearl Onions

Preparation time: 10 minutes
Cooking time: 6 hours and 5 minutes
Servings: 6

Ingredients:

- 3 pounds beef roast, trimmed and boneless
- 1 tablespoon Italian seasoning
- Black pepper to the taste
- 1 garlic clove, minced
- 1/3 cup sun-dried tomatoes, chopped
- ½ cup low sodium beef stock
- ½ cup kalamata olives pitted and halved
- 1 cup pearl onions
- 1 tablespoon olive oil

Directions:

1. Heat up a pan with the oil over medium high heat, add beef, brown for 5 minutes, take off heat and season with black pepper and Italian spices.
2. Transfer to your slow cooker, add tomatoes, onions and stock, cover and cook on Low for 6 hours.
3. Transfer to a cutting board, slice, divide between plates, add onions and tomatoes on the side and serve with cooking juices drizzled all over!

Enjoy!

Nutrition: calories 300, fat 5, fiber 5, carbs 8, protein 12

Light Beef

Preparation time: 10 minutes
Cooking time: 4 hours and 10 minutes
Servings: 4

Ingredients:
- 2 tablespoons olive oil
- 8 ounces mushrooms, sliced
- 1 yellow onion, chopped
- 2 pounds beef meat, cubed
- 1 cup veggie stock
- 14 ounces canned tomatoes, chopped
- ½ cup tomato sauce
- ¼ cup balsamic vinegar
- ½ cup garlic cloves, minced
- 1 can black olives, pitted and sliced
- 2 tablespoons rosemary, chopped
- 2 tablespoon parsley, chopped
- 1 tablespoon capers
- Black pepper to the taste

Directions:
1. Heat up a pan with half of the oil over medium high heat, add mushrooms, cook for 3-4 minutes stirring all the time and transfer them to your slow cooker.
2. Heat up the pan again over medium heat, add onion, stir, sauté for 3-4 minutes and add to slow cooker as well.
3. Heat up the pan once more over medium high heat, add meat, brown it for 10 minutes and add to slow cooker.
4. Add stock, tomatoes, tomato sauce, vinegar, garlic, olives, parsley, capers, black pepper and rosemary, stir gently, cover and cook on High for 4 hours.
5. Divide between plates and serve right away!

Enjoy!

Nutrition: calories 300, fat 4, fiber 3, carbs 6, protein 10

Perfect Beef And Eggplants

Preparation time: 10 minutes
Cooking time: 8 hours and 10 minutes
Servings: 6

Ingredients:
- 2 pounds beef, cubed
- 2 garlic cloves, minced
- 2 yellow onions, chopped
- 8 medium eggplants, cubed
- ¼ cup olive oil
- 1 pound tomato sauce
- 1 cup veggie stock
- 1 tablespoon balsamic vinegar
- 1/8 teaspoon allspice
- A pinch of cloves, ground
- ¼ cup parsley, chopped
- Black pepper to the taste
- A pinch of sea salt

Directions:
1. Heat up a pan with half of the oil over high heat, add meat, brown it for 5 minutes and transfer to your slow cooker.
2. Heat up the pan with the rest of the oil over medium heat, add eggplant pieces, garlic and onions, stir, cook for 4 minutes and add to slow cooker.
3. Also add stock, tomato sauce, vinegar, a pinch of salt, pepper, allspice and cloves, stir, cover and cook on Low for 8 hours.
4. Add parsley, stir gently, divide between plates and serve!

Nutrition: calories 353, fat 4, fiber 6, carbs 8, protein 10

Mediterranean Lamb

Preparation time: 10 minutes
Cooking time: 9 hours
Servings: 5

Ingredients:

- 1 pound lamb loin, cubed
- 2 garlic cloves, minced
- 1 teaspoon ginger, grated
- 1 red onion, chopped
- 1 teaspoon turmeric, ground
- ½ teaspoon cinnamon, ground
- 1 tablespoon honey
- 2 teaspoon cumin, ground
- 2 teaspoons coconut sugar
- 14 ounces canned tomatoes, crushed
- 1 cup low sodium chicken stock
- 1 cinnamon stick
- Black pepper to the taste
- 10 prunes, pitted
- ¼ lemon, peeled and chopped
- 3 tablespoons tapioca flour
- 1 tablespoon parsley, chopped
- 1 tablespoon coriander, chopped

Directions:

1. Put lamb meat in your slow cooker.
2. Add garlic, ginger, onion, turmeric, cinnamon, cumin, honey, sugar, tomatoes, chicken stock, cinnamon stick, a pinch of salt and pepper, stir gently, cover and cook on Low for 8 hours and 30 minutes.
3. Add prunes, lemon, tapioca flour, parsley and coriander, stir, cover and cook on Low for 30 minutes more.
4. Divide into bowls and serve.

Nutrition: calories 360, fat 4, fiber 6, carbs 8, protein 15

Rich Lamb Delight

Preparation time: 10 minutes
Cooking time: 8 hours and 10 minutes
Servings: 6

Ingredients:

- 3 pounds lamb shoulder, boneless
- 3 onions, roughly chopped
- 1 tablespoon olive oil
- 1 tablespoon oregano, chopped
- 6 garlic cloves, minced
- 1 tablespoon lemon zest, grated
- A pinch of sea salt
- Black pepper to the taste
- ½ teaspoon allspice
- 2 tablespoons tapioca flour
- 1 and ½ cups veggie stock
- 14 ounces canned artichoke hearts, chopped
- ¼ cup tomato paste
- 2 tablespoons parsley, chopped

Directions:

1. Heat up a pan with the oil over medium high heat, add lamb, brown for 5 minutes on each side and transfer to your slow cooker.
2. Heat up the pan again over medium high heat, add onion, lemon zest, garlic, a pinch of salt, pepper, oregano and allspice and cook for 5 minutes stirring often.
3. Add tapioca flour, stock and tomato paste, stir, bring to a boil over and pour over lamb.
4. Cover and cook on Low for 8 hours.
5. After 7 hours and 45 minutes add artichokes and parsley, stir gently, cover and cook on Low for 15 more minutes.
6. Divide into bowls and serve hot.

Nutrition: calories 370, fat 4, fiber 5, carbs 7, protein 16

Pork Shoulder

Preparation time: 10 minutes
Cooking time: 7 hours
Servings: 4

Ingredients:

- 2 and ½ pounds pork shoulder
- 4 cups chicken stock
- ½ cup coconut aminos
- ¼ cup white vinegar
- 2 tablespoons chili sauce
- Juice from 1 lime
- 1 tablespoon ginger, grated
- 1 tablespoon Chinese 5 spice
- 2 cup by portabella mushrooms, sliced
- A pinch of salt and black pepper
- 1 zucchini, sliced

Directions:

1. In your slow cooker, mix pork shoulder with stock, aminos, vinegar, chili sauce, lime juice, ginger, 5 spice, mushrooms, zucchini, salt and pepper, toss a bit, cover and cook on Low for 7 hours.
2. Transfer pork shoulder to a cutting board, shred using 2 forks, return to Crockpot and toss with the rest of the ingredients.
3. Divide pork between plates and serve.

Enjoy!

Nutrition: calories 342, fat 6, fiber 8, carbs 27, protein 18

Flavored Beef

Preparation time: 10 minutes
Cooking time: 6 hours
Servings: 4

Ingredients:

- 4 cups cauliflower rice, steamed
- 2 pound beef chuck roast
- 1 poblano pepper, chopped
- 6 ounces tomato paste
- 1 white onion, chopped
- 1 cup beef stock
- 2 tablespoons cumin, ground
- 2 tablespoons olive oil
- 1 tablespoon garlic, minced
- 1 tablespoon oregano, chopped
- 1 tablespoon smoked paprika
- ½ cup cilantro, chopped
- Lime wedges for serving

Directions:

1. In your slow cooker, mix oil with a beef roast, poblano pepper, tomato paste, onion, stock, cumin, garlic, oregano and smoked paprika, toss well, cover and cook on Low for 6 hours.
2. Slice meat, divide between plates and serve with cauliflower rice on the side, cilantro, sprinkled on top and lime wedges.

Enjoy!

Nutrition: calories 345, fat 7, fiber 8, carbs 18, protein 20

American Roast

Preparation time: 10 minutes
Cooking time: 8 hours
Servings: 4

Ingredients:

- 5 pounds beef chuck roast
- 1 tablespoon coconut aminos
- 10 pepperoncini
- 1 cup beef stock
- 2 tablespoons ghee

Directions:

1. In your slow cooker, mix beef roast with aminos, pepperoncini, stock and ghee, toss well, cover and cook on Low for 8 hours.
2. Transfer roast to a cutting board, shred using 2 forks, return to pot, toss, divide between plates and serve with a side salad.

Enjoy!

Nutrition: calories 362, fat 4, fiber 8, carbs 17, protein 17

Beef Chili

Preparation time: 10 minutes
Cooking time: 6 hours
Servings: 6

Ingredients:

- 2 pounds beef, ground
- 4 garlic cloves, minced
- 1 yellow onion, chopped
- 1 red bell pepper, chopped
- 1 green bell pepper, chopped
- 2 celery stalks, chopped
- ¼ cup green chilies, chopped
- 1 tomato, chopped
- 28 ounces canned tomatoes, crushed
- 14 ounces tomato sauce
- 2 tablespoons chili powder
- 1 tablespoons oregano, chopped
- ½ tablespoon basil, chopped
- ½ tablespoons cumin, ground
- ½ tablespoon adobo sauce
- A pinch of salt and black pepper
- A pinch of cayenne pepper

Directions:

1. In your instant pot, mix beef with garlic, onion, red bell pepper, green bell pepper, celery, chilies, tomato, crushed tomatoes, tomato sauce, chili powder, oregano, basil, cumin, adobo sauce, salt, pepper and cayenne, stir, cover and cook on Low for 6 hours.
2. Divide into bowls and serve.

Enjoy!

Nutrition: calories 372, fat 7, fiber 8, carbs 17, protein 16

Beef Stew

Preparation time: 10 minutes
Cooking time: 8 hours
Servings: 4

Ingredients:

- 2 cups beef stock
- 2 pounds beef stew meat
- 1 tablespoon balsamic vinegar
- 1 yellow onion, chopped
- 2 celery stalks, chopped
- 2 carrots, chopped
- 3 garlic cloves, minced
- 3 bay leaves
- 1 tablespoon sweet paprika
- A pinch of salt and black pepper
- 1 teaspoon rosemary, dried
- 1 teaspoon basil, dried
- 1 teaspoon oregano, dried
- 1/8 cup arrowroot powder

Directions:

1. In your slow cooker, mix beef stock with beef meat, vinegar, onion, celery, carrots, garlic, bay leaves, paprika, salt, pepper, rosemary, basil oregano and arrowroot powder, stir, cover and cook on Low for 8 hours.
2. Divide into bowls and serve hot.

Enjoy!

Nutrition: calories 327, fat 4, fiber 7, carbs 18, protein 8

Lamb Stew

Preparation time: 10 minutes
Cooking time: 8 hours
Servings: 6

Ingredients:

- 1 and ½ pound lamb steak, cubed
- 1 yellow onion, chopped
- 1 tablespoon olive oil
- 1 carrot, sliced
- A pinch of salt and black pepper
- 1 teaspoon lemon zest, grated
- 1 teaspoon cinnamon powder
- 1 and ½ teaspoon coriander seed powder
- 1 and ½ teaspoon cumin powder
- ½ teaspoon allspice
- 2 tablespoons lemon juice
- 1 teaspoon onion powder
- 2 garlic cloves, minced
- 7 apricots, dried and sliced
- 1 tablespoon tomato paste
- 2 bay leaves
- 1 and ½ cups water
- ¼ cup almonds, toasted
- 1 tablespoon parsley, chopped

Directions:

1. In your slow cooker, mix lamb with onion, oil, carrot, salt, pepper, lemon zest, cinnamon, coriander, cumin, allspice, lemon juice, onion powder, garlic, apricots, tomato paste, bay leaves and water, toss well, cover and cook on Low for 8 hours.
2. Add almonds and parsley, toss, divide into bowls and serve.

Enjoy!

Nutrition: calories 300, fat 4, fiber 8, carbs 17, protein 15

Beef Cheeks

Preparation time: 10 minutes
Cooking time: 4 hours
Servings: 4

Ingredients:

- 4 beef cheeks, halved
- 2 tablespoons coconut oil
- A pinch of salt and black pepper
- 1 white onion, chopped
- 4 garlic cloves, minced
- 2 cup beef stock
- 5 cardamom pods
- 1 tablespoon balsamic vinegar
- 3 bay leaves
- 7 cloves
- 2 vanilla beans, split
- 1 and ½ tablespoons tomato paste
- 1 carrot, sliced

Directions:

1. In your slow cooker, mix beef cheeks with melted coconut oil, salt, pepper, onion, garlic, stock, cardamom, vinegar, bay leaves, cloves, vanilla beans, tomato paste and carrot, toss, cover and cook on High for 4 hours.
2. Divide between plates and serve.

Enjoy!

Nutrition: calories 321, fat 5, fiber 7, carbs 18, protein 12

Beef and Veggies

Preparation time: 10 minutes
Cooking time: 8 hours
Servings: 6

Ingredients:

- 4 pounds beef roast
- 2 cups beef stock
- 2 sweet potatoes, cubed
- 6 carrots, sliced
- 7 celery stalks, chopped
- 1 yellow onion, chopped
- 1 tablespoon onion powder
- 1 tablespoon garlic powder
- 1 tablespoon sweet paprika
- A pinch of salt and black pepper

Directions:

1. In your slow cooker, beef with stock, sweet potatoes, carrots, celery, onion, onion powder, garlic powder, paprika, salt and pepper, stir, cover and cook on Low for 8 hours.
2. Slice roast, divide on plates, drizzle sauce from the pot all and serve with the veggies on the side.

Enjoy!

Nutrition: calories 372, fat 6, fiber 12, carbs 19, protein 11

Tasty Ham Soup

Preparation time: 10 minutes
Cooking time: 7 hours
Servings: 6

Ingredients:

- 1 ham bone with meat
- 10 cups water
- 2 tablespoons apple cider vinegar
- 3 bay leaves
- 1 Serrano pepper, chopped
- 2 tablespoons avocado oil
- 2 leeks, chopped
- 1 yellow onion, chopped
- 4 garlic cloves, minced
- 1 sweet potato, cubed
- 2 celery stalks, chopped
- 2 carrots, chopped
- 2 turnips, chopped
- ½ Savoy cabbage head, cut into medium strips
- 1 tablespoon thyme, chopped
- 1 handful parsley, chopped
- 1 teaspoon cumin, ground
- A pinch of salt and black pepper

Directions:

1. In your slow cooker, mix ham bone with water, vinegar, bay leaves, Serrano pepper, oil, leeks, onion, garlic, sweet potato, celery, carrots, turnips, cabbage, thyme, parsley, cumin, salt and pepper, stir, cover and cook on High for 5 hours.
2. Discard bone, return meat to pot, cover and cook on High for 2 more hours.
3. Divide soup into bowls and serve.

Enjoy!

Nutrition: calories 333, fat 8, fiber 12, carbs 19, protein 12

Beef Soup

Preparation time: 10 minutes
Cooking time: 6 hours
Servings: 4

Ingredients:

- 1 pound beef, ground
- 2 cups cauliflower, chopped
- 1 cup yellow onion, chopped
- 2 red bell peppers, chopped
- 15 ounces tomato sauce
- 15 ounces tomatoes, chopped
- 3 cups beef stock
- ½ teaspoon basil, dried
- ½ teaspoon oregano, dried
- 3 garlic cloves, minced
- A pinch of salt and black pepper

Directions:

1. In your slow cooker, mix beef with cauliflower, onion, bell peppers, tomato sauce, tomatoes, stock, basil, oregano, garlic, salt and pepper, stir, cover and cook on Low for 6 hours.
2. Stir soup one more time, ladle into bowls and serve.

Enjoy!

Nutrition: calories 214, fat 6, fiber 6, carbs 18, protein 7

Thai Pork Stew

Preparation time: 10 minutes
Cooking time: 7 hours
Servings: 4

Ingredients:

- 2 tablespoons olive oil
- 2 pounds pork butt, boneless and cubed
- A pinch of salt and black pepper to the taste
- 6 eggs, hard boiled, peeled and sliced
- 1 tablespoon cilantro, chopped
- 1 tablespoon coriander seeds
- 1 tablespoon ginger, grated
- 1 tablespoon black peppercorns
- 2 tablespoons garlic, chopped
- 2 tablespoons 5 spice powder
- 1 and ½ cup coconut aminos
- 2 tablespoons cocoa powder
- 1 yellow onion, chopped
- 8 cups water

Directions:

1. In your slow cooker, mix oil with pork cubes, salt, pepper, cilantro, coriander, ginger, peppercorns, garlic, 5 spice, aminos, cocoa, onion and water, toss, cover and cook on Low for 7 hours.
2. Divide stew into bowls, add egg slices on top and serve.

Enjoy!

Nutrition: calories 400, fat 10, fiber 9, carbs 28, protein 22

Asian Style Ribs

Preparation time: 10 minutes
Cooking time: 6 hours
Servings: 6

Ingredients:

- 4 pounds beef short ribs
- ½ cup beef stock
- ½ cup coconut aminos
- 2 tablespoons apple cider vinegar
- 1 tablespoon ginger, grated
- 4 garlic cloves, minced
- 1 tablespoon green onions, chopped
- 1 teaspoon sesame seeds

Directions:

1. In your slow cooker, mix ribs with stock, aminos, vinegar, ginger, garlic and green onions, stir, cover and cook on Low for 6 hours.
2. Add sesame seeds, toss, divide between plates and serve with cooking juices from the Crockpot drizzled all over.

Enjoy!

Nutrition: calories 349, fat 8, fiber 12, carbs 19, protein 4

Beef and Dill

Preparation time: 10 minutes
Cooking time: 5 hours
Servings: 6

Ingredients:
- 4 pounds beef brisket
- 2 oranges, sliced
- 2 garlic cloves, minced
- 2 yellow onions, thinly sliced
- 11 ounces celery, thinly sliced
- 1 tablespoon dill, dried
- 3 bay leaves
- 4 cinnamon sticks, cut into halves
- Salt and black pepper to the taste
- 17 ounces veggie stock

Directions:
1. In your slow cooker, mix beef with orange slices, garlic, onion, celery, dill, bay leaves, cinnamon, salt, pepper and stock, stir, cover and cook on High for 5 hours.
2. Divide beef mix between plates and serve.

Enjoy!

Nutrition: calories 300, fat 5, fiber 7, carbs 12, protein 4

Beef Curry

Preparation time: 10 minutes
Cooking time: 4 hours
Servings: 4

Ingredients:
- 2 pounds beef steak, cubed
- 2 tablespoons olive oil
- 1 tablespoon mustard
- 2 and ½ tablespoons curry powder
- 2 yellow onions, chopped
- 2 garlic cloves, minced
- 10 ounces canned coconut milk
- 2 tablespoons tomato sauce
- Salt and black pepper to the taste

Directions:
1. In your slow cooker, mix beef with oil, mustard, curry powder, onion, garlic, tomato paste, salt and pepper, stir, cover and cook on High for 3 hours and 40 minutes.
2. Add coconut milk, stir, cook on High for 20 minutes more, divide into bowls and serve.

Enjoy!

Nutrition: calories 400, fat 18, fiber 7, carbs 18, protein 22

Creamy Beef

Preparation time: 10 minutes
Cooking time: 5 hours
Servings: 4

Ingredients:

- 10 pounds beef, cubed
- 1 yellow onion, chopped
- 2 and ½ tablespoons olive oil
- 2 garlic cloves, minced
- 4 ounces mushrooms, sliced
- 1 and ½ tablespoon tomato paste
- Salt and black pepper to the taste
- 13 ounces beef stock
- 8 ounces coconut cream

Directions:

1. In your slow cooker, mix beef with onion, oil, garlic, mushrooms, tomato paste, salt, pepper, beef stock and coconut cream, stir, cover and cook on High for 5 hours.
2. Divide everything between plates and serve.

Enjoy!

Nutrition: calories 383, fat 7, fiber 6, carbs 22, protein 16

Winter Beef and Mushrooms

Preparation time: 10 minutes
Cooking time: 7 hours
Servings: 4

Ingredients:

- 3.5 ounces button mushrooms, sliced
- 3.5 ounces shiitake mushrooms, sliced
- 2 pounds beef shoulder, cut into medium cubes
- 16 ounces shallots, chopped
- 9 ounces beef stock
- 2 garlic cloves, minced
- 2 tablespoons chives, chopped
- 1 teaspoon sage, dried
- 1/8 teaspoon thyme, dried
- Salt and black pepper to the taste
- 3 and ½ tablespoons olive oil

Directions:

1. In your slow cooker, mix button mushrooms with shiitake mushrooms, beef, shallots, stock, garlic, chives, sage, thyme, salt, pepper and oil, toss, cover and cook on Low for 7 hours.
2. Divide beef and mushroom mix into plates and serve hot.

Enjoy!

Nutrition: calories 362, fat 7, fiber 4, carbs 17, protein 37

Beef Brisket Delight

Preparation time: 10 minutes
Cooking time: 8 hours
Servings: 6

Ingredients:

- 2 and ½ pounds beef brisket
- 4 cups veggie stock
- 2 bay leaves
- 3 garlic cloves, chopped
- 4 carrots, chopped
- 1 cabbage head cut into 6 wedges
- Salt and black pepper to the taste
- 3 turnips, cut into quarters

Directions:

1. In your slow cooker, mix beef with stock, bay leaves, garlic, carrots, cabbage, salt, pepper and turnips, stir, cover and cook on Low for 8 hours.
2. Divide beef brisket on plates and serve.

Enjoy!

Nutrition: calories 321, fat 15, fiber 4, carbs 18, protein 19

Tender Lamb Shanks

Preparation time: 10 minutes
Cooking time: 7 hours
Servings: 4

Ingredients:

- 4 lamb shanks
- 2 tablespoons olive oil
- 1 yellow onion, finely chopped
- 3 carrots, roughly chopped
- 2 garlic cloves, minced
- 2 tablespoons tomato paste
- 1 teaspoon oregano, dried
- 1 tomato, roughly chopped
- 4 ounces chicken stock
- Salt an black pepper to the taste

Directions:

1. In your slow cooker, mix lamb with oil, onion, garlic, carrots, tomato paste, tomato, oregano, stock, salt and pepper, stir, cover and cook on Low for 7 hours.
2. Divide into bowls and serve hot.

Enjoy!

Nutrition: calories 400, fat 13, fiber 4, carbs 17, protein 24

Lamb and Mushrooms

Preparation time: 10 minutes
Cooking time: 8 hours
Servings: 8

Ingredients:

- 1 and ½ pounds lamb leg, bone-in
- 2 carrots, sliced
- ½ pounds mushrooms, sliced
- 4 tomatoes, chopped
- 1 small yellow onion, chopped
- 6 garlic cloves, minced
- 2 tablespoons tomato paste
- 1 teaspoon olive oil
- Salt and black pepper to the taste
- A handful parsley, chopped

Directions:

1. In your slow cooker, mix lamb with carrots, mushrooms, tomatoes, onion, garlic, tomato paste, oil, salt, pepper and parsley, toss, cover and cook on Low for 8 hours.
2. Divide lamb mix between plates and serve.

Enjoy!

Nutrition: calories 372, fat 12, fiber 7, carbs 18, protein 22

Smoked Lamb Chops

Preparation time: 10 minutes
Cooking time: 7 hours
Servings: 4

Ingredients:

- 4 lamb chops
- 1 teaspoon liquid smoke
- 1 cup green onions, chopped
- 2 cups canned tomatoes, chopped
- 1 teaspoon smoked paprika
- 2 tablespoons garlic, minced
- Salt and black pepper to the taste
- 3 cups beef stock

Directions:

1. In your slow cooker, mix lamb with liquid smoke, green onions, tomatoes, paprika, garlic, salt, pepper and stock, stir, cover and cook on Low for 7 hours.
2. Divide everything between plates and serve.

Enjoy!

Nutrition: calorie 364, fat 12, fiber 7, carbs 29, protein 28

Creamy Pork Chops and Onion Sauce

Preparation time: 10 minutes
Cooking time: 5 hours
Servings: 4

Ingredients:

- 4 pork chops
- 2 tablespoons parsley, chopped
- 1 garlic clove, minced
- 2 tablespoons lime juice
- 2 tablespoons olive oil
- 1 pound onions, sliced
- ½ cup coconut milk
- Salt and black pepper to the taste

Directions:

1. In your slow cooker, mix pork chops with garlic, lime juice, oil, onions, salt and pepper, stir, cover and cook on Low for 4 hours and 40 minutes.
2. Add parsley and coconut milk, stir, cover and cook on High for 20 minutes more.
3. Divide pork chops between plates and serve them with the creamy onion sauce on the side.

Enjoy!

Nutrition: calories 243, fat 7, fiber 9, carbs 12, protein 22

Ribs and Apple Sauce

Preparation time: 10 minutes
Cooking time: 6 hours
Servings: 4

Ingredients:

- 2 and ½ pounds baby back ribs
- 1 teaspoon onion powder
- 1 teaspoon paprika
- ½ teaspoon dry mustard
- ½ teaspoon chili powder
- ½ teaspoon garlic powder
- 1 small yellow onion, chopped
- 2 bacon slices, chopped
- 6 ounces tomato paste
- ¾ cup tomato sauce
- 2 garlic cloves, minced
- Salt and black pepper to the taste
- ¼ cup coconut aminos
- 1/3 cup apple cider vinegar
- 1 tablespoon olive oil
- ½ cup apple juice

Directions:

1. In your slow cooker, mix baby back ribs with onion powder, paprika, mustard powder, chili powder and garlic powder and rub well.
2. Add onion, bacon, tomato paste and sauce, garlic, salt, pepper, aminos, vinegar, oil and apple juice, toss well, cover and cook on Low for 6 hours.
3. Divide ribs and sauce between plates and serve them hot.

Enjoy!

Nutrition: calories 300, fat 12, fiber 4, carbs 10, protein 14

Slow Cooked Sausages and Sauce

Preparation time: 15 minutes
Cooking time: 3 hours
Servings: 6

Ingredients:

- 6 pork sausages
- 2 tablespoons olive oil
- ½ cup onion jam
- 3 ounces beef stock
- 3 ounces water
- Salt and black pepper to the taste
- 1 tablespoon tapioca flour

Directions:

1. In your slow cooker, mix sausages with oil, onion jam, stock, water, salt, pepper and tapioca flour, toss, cover and cook on High for 3 hours.
2. Divide sausage and sauce between plates and serve.

Enjoy!

Nutrition: calories 431, fat 15, fiber 4, carbs 29, protein 13

Greek Lamb

Preparation time: 15 minutes
Cooking time: 7 hours
Servings: 4

Ingredients:

- 6-pound lamb leg, boneless
- 2 tablespoons olive oil
- Salt and black pepper to the taste
- 1 bay leaf
- 1 teaspoon marjoram
- 1 teaspoon sage, dried
- 1 teaspoon ginger, grated
- 3 garlic cloves, minced
- 1 teaspoon thyme, dried
- 2 cups veggie stock

Directions:

1. In your slow cooker, mix lamb with oil, salt, pepper, bay leaf, marjoram, sage, ginger, garlic, thyme and stock, stir, cover and cook on Low for 7 hours.
2. Divide between plates and serve.

Enjoy!

Nutrition: calories 263, fat 8, fiber 9, carbs 12, protein 4

French Lamb Chops

Preparation time: 10 minutes
Cooking time: 8 hours
Servings: 4

Ingredients:
- 4 lamb chops
- 1 cup onion, chopped
- 2 cups canned tomatoes, chopped
- 1 cup leek, chopped
- 2 tablespoons garlic, minced
- 1 teaspoon herbs de Provence
- Salt and black pepper to the taste
- 3 cups water

Directions:
1. In your slow cooker mix, lamb chops with onion, tomatoes, leek, garlic, herbs de Provence, salt, pepper and water, stir, cover and cook on Low for 8 hours.
2. Divide lamb and veggies between plates and serve.

Enjoy!

Nutrition: calories 430, fat 12, fiber 8, carbs 20, protein 18

Paleo Slow Cooker Dessert Recipes

Sweet Cookies

Preparation time: 10 minutes
Cooking time: 2 hours and 30 minutes
Servings: 12

Ingredients:

- 1 egg white
- ¼ cup coconut oil, melted
- 1 cup coconut sugar
- ½ teaspoon vanilla extract
- 1 teaspoon baking powder
- 1 and ½ cups almond meal
- ½ cup dark chocolate chips

Directions:

1. In a bowl, mix coconut oil with sugar, vanilla extract and egg white and beat well using your mixer.
2. Add baking powder and almond meal and stir well.
3. Fold in chocolate chips and stir gently.
4. Line your slow cooker with parchment paper and grease it a bit.
5. Transfer cookie mix to the slow cooker and press it well on the bottom.
6. Cover and cook on low for 2 hours and 30 minutes.
7. Take cookie sheet put of the slow cooker using the parchment paper as a handle.
8. Cut into 12 bars and serve cold.

Enjoy!

Nutrition: calories 220, fat 2, fiber 1, carbs 3, protein 6

Glazed Pecans

Preparation time: 10 minutes
Cooking time: 2 hours
Servings: 5

Ingredients:

- 2 teaspoons vanilla extract
- 3 cups pecans
- ¼ cup maple syrup
- 1 tablespoon coconut oil

Directions:

1. Put your pecans in the slow cooker.
2. Add vanilla extract, oil and maple syrup, toss to coat and cook on Low for 2 hours.
3. Divide into small cups and serve.

Enjoy!

Nutrition: calories 120, fat 2, fiber 2, carbs 4, protein 7

Simple Poached Pears

Preparation time: 10 minutes
Cooking time: 4 hours
Servings: 4

Ingredients:
- 4 pears, peeled and tops cut off and cored
- 5 cardamom pods
- 2 cups orange juice
- ¼ cup maple syrup
- 1 cinnamon stick
- 1 inch ginger, grated

Directions:
1. Put the pears in your slow cooker.
2. Add cardamom pods, orange juice, maple syrup, cinnamon and ginger, cover and cook on Low for 4 hours.
3. Divide pears between plates and serve with the orange sauce on top.

Enjoy!

Nutrition: calories 200, fat 0, fiber 2, carbs 3, protein 4

Rich Stuffed Apples

Preparation time: 10 minutes
Cooking time: 1 hour and 30 minutes
Servings: 5

Ingredients:
- 5 apples, tops cut off and cored
- 5 figs
- 1/3 cup coconut sugar
- 1 teaspoon dried ginger
- ¼ cup pecans, chopped
- 2 teaspoons lemon zest, grated
- ¼ teaspoon nutmeg
- ½ teaspoon cinnamon
- 1 tablespoon lemon juice
- 1 tablespoon coconut oil
- ½ cup water

Directions:
1. In a bowl, mix figs with sugar, ginger, pecans, lemon zest, nutmeg, cinnamon, oil and lemon juice, whisk really well and stuff your apples with this mix.
2. Put the water in your slow cooker, arrange apples inside, cover and cook on High for 1 hour and 30 minutes.
3. Divide onto dessert plates and serve.

Enjoy!

Nutrition: calories 200, fat 1, fiber 2, carbs 4, protein 7

Chocolate Cake

Preparation time: 10 minutes
Cooking time: 3 hours
Servings: 10

Ingredients:

- 1 cup almond flour
- 3 tablespoons egg white protein powder
- ½ cup cocoa powder
- ½ cup swerve
- 1 and ½ teaspoons baking powder
- 3 eggs
- 4 tablespoons coconut oil, melted
- ¾ teaspoon vanilla extract
- 2/3 cup almond milk
- 1/3 cup dark chocolate chips

Directions:

1. In a bowl, mix swerve with almond flour, egg white protein, cocoa powder and baking powder and stir.
2. Add almond milk, oil, eggs, chocolate chips and vanilla extract and whisk really well.
3. Pour this into your lined and greased slow cooker and cook on Low for 2 hours.
4. Leave cake aside to cool down, slice and serve it.

Enjoy!

Nutrition: calories 200, fat 12, fiber 4, carbs 8, protein 6

Pumpkin Cake

Preparation time: 10 minutes
Cooking time: 2 hours and 15 minutes
Servings: 12

Ingredients:

- 1 and ½ teaspoons baking powder
- 2 cups almond flour
- ½ teaspoon baking soda
- ¼ teaspoon nutmeg, ground
- 1 and ½ teaspoons cinnamon, ground
- ¼ teaspoon ginger, ground
- 1 tablespoon coconut oil, melted
- 1 egg white
- 1 tablespoon vanilla extract
- 1 cup pumpkin puree
- 1/3 cup maple syrup
- 1 teaspoon lemon juice
- Cooking spray

Directions:

1. In a bowl, flour with baking powder, baking soda, cinnamon, ginger and nutmeg and stir.
2. In another bowl, mix oil with egg white, vanilla extract, pumpkin puree, maple syrup and lemon juice and stir well.
3. Combine flour mixture with butter mixture and stir well again.
4. Spray your slow cooker with cooking spray and line it with tin foil.
5. Pour cake mix into your slow cooker, spread, cover and cook on Low for 2 hours and 15 minutes.
6. Leave your cake to cool down, before slicing and serve it.

Enjoy!

Nutrition: calories 200, fat 3, fiber 2, carbs 6, protein 6

Orange Pudding

Preparation time: 10 minutes
Cooking time: 5 hours and 3 minutes
Servings: 4

Ingredients:

- Cooking spray
- 1 teaspoon baking powder
- 1 cup almond flour
- 1 cup palm sugar
- ½ teaspoon cinnamon, ground
- 3 tablespoons coconut oil, melted
- ½ cup almond milk
- ½ cup pecans, chopped
- ¾ cup water
- ½ cup raisins
- ½ cup orange peel, grated
- ¾ cup orange juice
- Chopped pecans for serving

Directions:

1. Spray your slow cooker with cooking spray.
2. In a bowl, mix flour with half of the sugar, baking powder and cinnamon and stir.
3. Add 2 tablespoons oil and milk and stir again well.
4. Add pecans and raisins, stir and pour this into slow cooker.
5. Heat up a small pan over medium high heat, add water, orange juice, orange peel, the rest of the oil and the remaining sugar, stir, bring to a boil, pour over the mix in the slow cooker, cover and cook on Low for 5 hours.
6. Divide into dessert bowls and serve with chopped pecans on top.

Enjoy!

Nutrition: calories 222, fat 3, fiber 1, carbs 8, protein 6

Apple Crisp

Preparation time: 10 minutes
Cooking time: 4 hours
Servings: 8

Ingredients:

- Cooking spray
- 2 teaspoons lemon juice
- 3 tablespoons coconut sugar
- ¼ teaspoon ginger, grated
- 1 and ½ teaspoons arrowroot powder
- 6 big apples, roughly chopped
- ½ cup almond flour
- ½ cup palm sugar
- 1/8 teaspoon nutmeg, ground
- ¼ teaspoon cinnamon powder
- ¼ cup coconut oil, melted
- ½ cup walnuts, chopped

Directions:

1. Spray your slow cooker with cooking spray.
2. In a bowl, mix coconut sugar with lemon juice, ginger, arrowroot powder, apples and cinnamon, stir and pour into your slow cooker.
3. In another bowl, mix flour with palm sugar, nutmeg, walnuts and oil and stir well.
4. Pour this over apple mix in the slow cooker, cover and cook on Low for 4 hours. Divide into bowls and serve!

Enjoy!

Nutrition: calories 180, fat 3, fiber 2, carbs 6, protein 5

Berry Cobbler

Preparation time: 10 minutes
Cooking time: 2 hours
Servings: 6

Ingredients:

- 1 pound fresh blackberries
- 1 pound fresh blueberries
- ¾ cup water
- ¾ cup coconut sugar
- ¾ cup almond flour
- ¼ cup tapioca flour
- ½ cup arrowroot powder
- 1 teaspoon baking powder
- 2 tablespoons palm sugar
- 1/3 cup almond milk
- 1 egg, whisked
- 1 teaspoon lemon zest, grated
- 3 tablespoons coconut oil, melted

Directions:

1. Put blueberries, blackberries, coconut sugar, water and tapioca in your slow cooker, cover and cook on High for 1 hour.
2. Meanwhile, in a bowl, mix flour with arrowroot, palm sugar and baking powder and stir well.
3. In a second bowl, mix the egg with milk, oil and lemon zest.
4. Combine egg mixture with flour mixture, stir well and drop tablespoons of this mix over the berries from the slow cooker.
5. Cover and cook on High for 1 more hour.
6. Leave cobbler aside to cool down, divide into dessert bowls and serve.

Enjoy!

Nutrition: calories 240, fat 4, fiber 3, carbs 6, protein 6

Special Dessert

Preparation time: 10 minutes
Cooking time: 1 hour and 30 minutes
Servings: 8

Ingredients:

- 1/3 cup coconut flour
- ½ teaspoon baking soda
- 3 eggs
- 5 tablespoons coconut oil
- 2 tablespoons honey

For the topping:

- 4 tablespoons coconut oil, melted
- 1 tablespoon cinnamon powder
- 1 cup honey

Directions:

1. In a bowl, mix flour with baking soda, eggs, 5 tablespoons coconut oil and 2 tablespoons honey, stir well until you obtain a dough and shape 8 balls out of it.
2. In a bowl, mix 4 tablespoons melted oil with cinnamon and 1 cup honey and whisk really well.
3. Dip balls into this mix and arrange them in your slow cooker.
4. Cover and cook on Low for 1 hour and 30 minutes.
5. Leave this Paleo dessert to cool down before serving it.

Enjoy!

Nutrition: calories 230, fat 2, fiber 4, carbs 6, protein 7

Apple Bread

Preparation time: 10 minutes
Cooking time: 2 hours and 20 minutes
Servings: 6

Ingredients:
- 3 cups apples, cored and cubed
- 1 cup coconut sugar
- 1 tablespoon vanilla
- 2 eggs
-
- 1 tablespoon apple pie spice
- 2 cups almond flour
- 1 tablespoon baking powder
- 1 tablespoon ghee

Directions:
1. In a bowl, mix apples with coconut sugar, vanilla, eggs, apple pie spice, almond flour, baking powder and ghee, whisk well, pour into your slow cooker, cover and cook on High for 2 hours and 20 minutes.
2. Leave sweet bread to cool down, slice and serve.

Enjoy!

Nutrition: calories 100, fat 2, fiber 4, carbs 12, protein 4

Banana Cake

Preparation time: 10 minutes
Cooking time: 2 hours
Servings: 6

Ingredients:
- ¾ cup coconut sugar
- 1/3 cup ghee, soft
- 1 teaspoon vanilla
- 1 egg
- 3 bananas, mashed
- 1 teaspoon baking powder
- 1 and ½ cups coconut flour
- ½ teaspoons baking soda
- 1/3 cup cashew milk
- Cooking spray

Directions:
1. In a bowl, mix ghee with coconut sugar, vanilla extract, eggs, mashed bananas, baking powder, coconut flour, baking soda and cashew milk and stir really well.
2. Grease your slow cooker with cooking spray, add cake batter, spread, cover and cook on High for 2 hours.
3. Leave cake to cool down, slice and serve.

Enjoy!

Nutrition: calories 300, fat 4, fiber 4, carbs 27, protein 4

Chocolate Pudding

Preparation time: 10 minutes
Cooking time: 1 hour
Servings: 4

Ingredients:
- 4 ounces coconut cream
- 4 ounces dark chocolate, cut into chunks
- 1 teaspoon coconut sugar

Directions:
1. In a bowl, mix coconut cream with chocolate and sugar, whisk really well, pour into your slow cooker, cover and cook on High for 1 hour.
2. Divide into bowls and serve cold.

Enjoy!

Nutrition: calories 232, fat 12, fiber 6, carbs 9, protein 4

Cauliflower Rice Pudding

Preparation time: 5 minutes
Cooking time: 2 hours
Servings: 6

Ingredients:
- 1 tablespoon ghee, melted
- 7 ounces cauliflower rice
- 4 ounces water
- 16 ounces coconut milk
- 3 ounces coconut sugar
- 1 egg
- 1 teaspoon cinnamon powder
- 1 teaspoon vanilla extract

Directions:
1. In your slow cooker, mix ghee with cauliflower rice, water, coconut milk, coconut sugar, egg, cinnamon and vanilla extract, stir, cover and cook on High for 2 hours.
2. Divide pudding into bowls and serve cold.

Enjoy!

Nutrition: calories 162, fat 2, fiber 6, carbs 18, protein 4

Avocado and Green Tea Dessert

Preparation time: 6 minutes
Cooking time: 1 hour
Servings: 4

Ingredients:

- ½ cup coconut water
- 1 and ½ cup avocado, chopped
- 2 tablespoons green tea powder
- 2 teaspoons lime zest, grated
- 1 tablespoon coconut sugar

Directions:

1. In your slow cooker, mix coconut water with avocado, green tea powder, lime zest and coconut sugar, stir, cover and cook on Low for 1 hour.
2. Divide into bowls and serve.

Enjoy!

Nutrition: calories 307, fat 4, fiber 8, carbs 11, protein 7

Pumpkin and Chia Pudding

Preparation time: 10 minutes
Cooking time: 1 hour
Servings: 4

Ingredients:

- 1 cup almond milk
- ½ cup pumpkin puree
- 2 tablespoons maple syrup
- ½ cup coconut milk
- ¼ cup chia seeds
- ½ teaspoon cinnamon powder
- ¼ teaspoon ginger, grated

Directions:

1. In your slow cooker, mix almond milk with coconut milk, pumpkin puree, maple syrup, chia, cinnamon and ginger, stir, cover and cook on High for 1 hour.
2. Divide pudding into bowls and serve.

Enjoy!

Nutrition: calories 105, fat 2, fiber 7, carbs 11, protein 4

Figs and Coconut Butter Dessert

Preparation time: 10 minutes
Cooking time: 1 hour
Servings: 4

Ingredients:

- 2 tablespoons coconut butter
- 12 figs, halved
- 1 cup almonds, chopped
- ¼ cup maple syrup

Directions:

1. In your slow cooker, mix coconut butter with maple syrup and whisk well.
2. Add figs and almonds, toss, cover and cook on Low for 1 hour.
3. Divide into bowls and serve warm.

Enjoy!

Nutrition: calories 200, fat 6, fiber 8, carbs 9, protein 12

Apples and Sweet Sauce

Preparation time: 10 minutes
Cooking time: 1 hour
Servings: 4

Ingredients:

- 4 green apples cored and cut into medium cubes
- 1 tablespoon pure maple syrup
- A pinch of cardamom
- ½ teaspoon cinnamon powder
- ½ teaspoon vanilla extract

Directions:

1. In your slow cooker, mix apples with maple syrup, cardamom, cinnamon and vanilla, stir, cover and cook on Low for 1 hour.
2. Divide into bowls and serve.

Enjoy!

Nutrition: calories 135, fat 1, fiber 3, carbs 4, protein 2

Grapefruit Compote

Preparation time: 10 minutes
Cooking time: 2 hours
Servings: 6

Ingredients:
- 1 cup water
- 1 cup maple syrup
- ½ cup mint, chopped
- 64 ounces red grapefruit juice
- 2 grapefruits, peeled and chopped

Directions:
1. In your slow cooker, mix grapefruit with water, maple syrup, mint and grapefruit juice, stir, cover and cook on High for 2 hours.
2. Divide into bowls and serve cold.

Enjoy!

Nutrition: 120, fat 1, fiber, 2, carbs 2, protein 1

Cherry Compote

Preparation time: 10 minutes
Cooking time: 2 hours
Servings: 6

Ingredients:
- ½ cup dark cocoa powder
- ¾ cup red cherry juice
- ¼ cup maple syrup
- 1 pound cherries, pitted and halved
- 2 tablespoons stevia
- 2 cups water

Directions:
1. In your slow cooker, mix cocoa powder with cherry juice, maple syrup, cherries, water and stevia, stir, cover and cook on High for 2 hours.
2. Divide into bowls and serve cold.

Enjoy!

Nutrition: calories 197, fat 1, fiber 4, carbs 5, protein 2

Passion Fruit Pudding

Preparation time: 10 minutes
Cooking time: 2 hours
Servings: 6

Ingredients:

- 1 cup passion fruit curd
- 4 passion fruits, pulp and seeds separated
- 3 and ½ ounces maple syrup
- 3 eggs
- 2 ounces ghee, melted
- 3 and ½ ounces almond milk
- ½ cup almond flour
- ½ teaspoon baking powder

Directions:

1. In your slow cooker, mix curd with passion fruits pulp and seeds, maple syrup, eggs, ghee, almond milk, almond flour and baking powder, whisk really well, cover and cook on High for 2 hours.
2. Divide into bowls and serve cold.

Enjoy!

Nutrition: calories 230, fat 12, fiber 3, carbs 7, protein 8

Cashew Cake

Preparation time: 10 minutes
Cooking time: 2 hours
Servings: 6

Ingredients:

For the crust:

- ½ cup dates, pitted
- 1 tablespoon water
- ½ teaspoon vanilla
- ½ cup almonds

For the cake:

- 2 and ½ cups cashews, soaked for 8 hours
- 1 cup blueberries
- ¾ cup maple syrup
- 1 tablespoon coconut oil

Directions:

1. In your food processor, mix dates with water, vanilla, almonds, and pulse well.
2. Transfer dough to a working surface, flatten it and arrange on the bottom of your slow cooker.
3. In your blender, mix maple syrup with coconut oil, cashews and blueberries, blend well, spread over crust, cover and cook on High for 2 hours.
4. Leave cake to cool down, slice and serve.

Enjoy!

Nutrition: calories 200, fat 3, fiber 5, carbs 12, protein 3

Lemon Pudding

Preparation time: 10 minutes
Cooking time: 1 hour
Servings: 4

Ingredients:
- 1/3 cup natural cashew butter
- 1 and ½ tablespoons coconut oil
- 2 tablespoons coconut butter
- 5 tablespoons lemon juice
- ½ teaspoon lemon zest
- 1 tablespoons maple syrup

Directions:
1. In a bowl, mix cashew butter with coconut butter, coconut oil, lemon juice, lemon zest and maple syrup and stir until you obtain a creamy mix.
2. Pour into your slow cooker, cook on High for 1 hour, divide into bowls and serve.

Enjoy!

Nutrition: calories 102, fat 4, fiber 0, carbs 4, protein 1

Pumpkin Cake

Preparation time: 10 minutes
Cooking time: 2 hours
Servings: 10

Ingredients:
- 1 and ½ teaspoons baking powder
- 2 cups coconut flour
- ½ teaspoon baking soda
- ¼ teaspoon nutmeg, ground
- 1 teaspoons cinnamon powder
- ¼ teaspoon ginger, grated
- 1 tablespoon coconut oil, melted
- 1 egg white
- 1 tablespoon vanilla extract
- 1 cup pumpkin puree
- 2 tablespoons stevia
- 1 teaspoon lemon juice

Directions:
1. In a bowl, flour with baking powder, baking soda, cinnamon, ginger, nutmeg, oil, egg white, ghee, vanilla extract, pumpkin puree, stevia and lemon juice, stir well and transfer this your slow cooker.
2. Cover, cook on High for 2 hours, leave aside to cool down, slice and serve.

Enjoy!

Nutrition: calories 180, fat 3, fiber 2, carbs 3, protein 4

Orange Pudding

Preparation time: 10 minutes
Cooking time: 1 hour
Servings: 4

Ingredients:

- 1 teaspoon baking powder
- 1 cup coconut flour
- 2 tablespoons stevia
- ½ teaspoon cinnamon powder
- 3 tablespoons coconut oil, melted
- ½ cup coconut milk
- ½ cup pecans, chopped
- ½ cup raisins
- ½ cup orange peel, grated
- ¾ cup orange juice

Directions:

1. In a bowl, mix flour with stevia, baking powder, cinnamon, 2 tablespoons oil, milk, pecans and raisins, stir and pour into your slow cooker
2. In a pan, mix orange juice, orange peel and the rest of the oil, stir, bring to a boil over medium heat and pour over the pecans mix.
3. Cover, cook on High for 1 hour, leave aside to cool down, slice and serve.

Enjoy!

Nutrition: calories 142, fat 3, fiber 1, carbs 3, protein 3

Fruits Mix

Preparation time: 10 minutes
Cooking time: 1 hour
Servings: 6

Ingredients:

- 1-quart water
- 2 tablespoons stevia
- 1 pound mixed apples and pears
- 5-star anise
- 2 cinnamon sticks
- Zest from 1 orange, grated
- Zest from 1 lemon, grated

Directions:

1. Put the water, stevia, apples, pears, star anise, cinnamon, orange and lemon zest in your slow cooker, cover and cook on High for 1 hour
2. Divide into bowls and serve cold.

Enjoy!

Nutrition: calories 98, fat 0, fiber 0, carbs 0, protein 2

Delicious Flavoured Apples

Preparation time: 10 minutes
Cooking time: 1 hour
Servings: 8

Ingredients:

- 1 teaspoon cinnamon powder
- 12 ounces apples, cored and chopped
- 2 tablespoons flax seed meal mixed with 1 tablespoon water
- ½ cup coconut cream
- 3 tablespoons stevia
- ½ teaspoon nutmeg
- 2 teaspoons vanilla extract
- 1/3 cup pecans, chopped

Directions:

1. In your slow cooker, mix flax seed meal with coconut cream, vanilla, nutmeg, stevia, apples and cinnamon, stir a bit, cover and cook on High for 1 hour.
2. Divide into bowls, sprinkle pecans on top and serve cold

Enjoy!

Nutrition: calories 120, fat 3, fiber 2, carbs 4, protein 3

Plum Compote

Preparation time: 10 minutes
Cooking time: 1 hour
Servings: 10

Ingredients:

- 4 pounds plums, stones removed and chopped
- 1 cup water
- 2 tablespoons stevia
- 1 teaspoon cinnamon powder

Directions:

1. Put plums, water, stevia and cinnamon in your slow cooker, cover and cook on High for 1 hour.
2. Divide bowls and serve cold.

Enjoy!

Nutrition: calories 103, fat 0, fiber 1, carbs 2, protein 4

Lemon Jam

Preparation time: 10 minutes
Cooking time: 2 hours
Servings: 8

Ingredients:
- 2 pounds lemons, sliced
- 2 cups dates
- 1 cup water
- 1 tablespoon vinegar
- 2 tablespoons coconut sugar

Directions:
1. Put dates in your blender, add water and pulse really well.
2. Put lemon slices in your slow cooker, add dates paste, sugar and vinegar, stir, cover and cook on Low for 2 hours
3. Divide into small jars and serve cold.

Enjoy!

Nutrition: calories 102, fat 2, fiber 1, carbs 2, protein 4

Apple Cake

Preparation time: 10 minutes
Cooking time: 2 hours and 30 minutes
Servings: 6

Ingredients:
- 3 cups apples, cored and cubed
- 3 tablespoons stevia
- 1 tablespoon vanilla extract
- 2 eggs
- 1 tablespoon apple pie spice
- 2 cups coconut flour
- 1 tablespoon baking powder
- 1 tablespoon ghee

Directions:
3. In a bowl mix eggs with ghee, apple pie spice, vanilla, apples and stevia and stir using your mixer.
4. In another bowl, mix baking powder with flour, stir, add to apple mix, stir again well and transfer to your slow cooker.
5. Cover, cook on High for 2 hours and 30 minutes, and leave cake aside to cool down, slice and serve.

Enjoy!

Nutrition: calories 130, fat 2, fiber 1, carbs 2, protein 4

Conclusion

A Paleo diet is extremely healthy and you should opt for it if you need to make a significant change in your life. In addition, slow cooking is one of the most popular cooking methods these days that allows you to prepare delicious dishes for you and your loved ones.

Slow cooking helps you make healthy meals in a very simple way.

So, why shouldn't you combine a healthy diet with slow cooking?

Trust us! The best thing you could do is to adopt a Paleo diet and to start cooking some of the most amazing Paleo recipes in your modern slow cooker!

What are you still waiting for? Get your hands on a copy of this incredible Paleo slow cooker cookbook and start your new life right away!

Have fun!

Recipe Index